The Principles Of Success

John S. Matthew

DEDICATION

This book is dedicated to my lovely mother (Of blessed memory) Mrs. Onyemarechi Samuel who taught me hard work as a child, and by whose gene I am able to keep my head up in the face of daunting challenges, and above the limitations of our environment. Mummy, I will always remember you for your impeccable character and success.

.

CONTENTS

ACKNOWLEDGMENTS

Authoring a book is not a drive-alone project where the author did everything single handedly as would in Robinson Crusoe's economy. This book has certainly received immense contributions from people. Therefore my first appreciation goes to God, the maker of heaven and earth who gave me the wisdom and courage to start and complete this project

Closely ranking next in my appreciation list is my primary and secondary-school-days' classmate and friend, Dr. Samuel Jeremiah who painstakingly read through the manuscripts, and made all necessary corrections and advice, bringing this book to stand in the midst of other good books. I sincerely appreciate him for blessing me, and indeed the readers with his wealth of knowledge.

My appreciation wouldn't be complete and meaningful without appreciating my lovely wife, Mrs. Chioma John for providing warmth and ambience for this odious task, and above all typing the entire manuscripts.

I also want to appreciate Mr. Friday Okporo, my dear friend; Mr. Godfirst Matthew, my cousin for their immense assistance with their offices because of steady power supply during proof-reading and correction. Also appreciated are Pst. Celestine Chabaand, Mr.

Atoukaritou N. Sasime for helping with Bible quotations, and a host of well-meaning friends and family members whom are impossible to mention one by one- I owe you greatly for this success.

.

INTRODUCTION

Evidently there is ever growing need to be successful in our chosen careers and endeavors today than before.

Also growing is the number of people who want, or wish to be successful in their lives generally, or particularly rich in the financial aspect so could be famous as Bill Gates or Warren Buffet.

The reason for this trend may not be far from the increase in demand on excellence and knowledge by our society, even with the harsh economic reality-people need to pay the auto loan, medical bills and the mortgages that seem to suddenly fall due.

Whatever the reason for the trend, we need to know what needs to be done, and be prepared to do in order to get out of this quagmire.

On this premise, *The Principles of Success* is invaluable, and recommended as a-must-read for every genuine seeker of success, irrespective of field; the principles are widely applicable.

It starts with general overview of success in chapter

one, and later takes a perspective, and then provides a foundation for achieving success.

This book tries to give clear picture of what is means to be successful by examining success from various dictionary definitions, and narrow it down to definite perspective and dwells on it.

It delves into the intricacies of creating success: the foundation, the ability to identify success before it materializes; the power of goal and vision, the indispensability of platform creation and more.

Also in the pages of this book will be exposed the subtlety and sneaking inertia that culminates into procrastination, the clog in wheel of success.
With the help of this book you will be able to see through the popular misconception of IQ and degrees as the basics for success, especially financial prosperity.

The author has studied a couple of successful persons from career to career, race to race, nationality to nationality and even different generations and has summarized it into this volume – the revelations that will open you up and encourage you to be a better and successful person!

Until we clearly see these misconceptions and myths, achieving success would never stop seeming illusory. But thank God you have found this book to help unravel and dispel those misconception – especially intertwining success with degrees and IQ, so you too can feel qualified to be successful in your career, becoming rich financially even without those purported degrees and high IQ necessities.

One last word: It emphasizes and compels you to take action, as the catalyst for success. Good luck!

JOHN S. MATTHEW

Chapter One

WHAT IS SUCCESS?

It is important and pragmatic to begin a crucial subject as this with its meaning.

Success: The Oxford Advanced Learner's Dictionary defines it thus

1)   "The fact that you have achieved something that you want and have been trying to do or get; the fact of becoming rich or famous or getting high social position".

2) "A person or thing that has achieved a good result and been successful"

Let's consider the meaning from another dictionary: Encarta Dictionary. It defines it thus:

1)   Achievement of intention: "The achievement of something planned or attempted"

2)   Attainment of fame, wealth or power: "impressive achievement, especially the achievement of fame, wealth or power".

3)   Something that turns out well: "Something that

turns out as planned or intended".

4) Somebody successful: "Somebody who is wealthy, famous, or powerful because of a record or achievement".

From the above definitions, you can easily understand that success is fairly general but could be classified into the following classes.

i) Success resulting from achievement of desired goal. (irrespective of the goal)

ii) Success resulting from attainment of riches or high social position-status

iii) Success resulting from attainment of good result.

Let me expatiate on the three categories of success as itemized above:

Success resulting from achievement of desired goal; e.g a person who wants to train himself/herself, or children in particular way; achievement of any worthy objective: winning a contest or an election, graduating from school with desired grade etc.

Next is success resulting from attainment of riches or high social recognition; the people in this class are the world millionaires and billionaires like: Bill Gates, the world richest; AmancioOtega, the world second richest

(2016); Warren Buffet, the world third richest (2016); Carlos Slim, the fourth richest (2016) ;Jeff Bezos, the fifth richest (2016) , and Aliko Dangote etc. Still under this category are the world leaders like Abraham Lincoln, Barrack Obama, Nelson Mandela etc;the inventors and scientists: Thomas Edison, Henry Ford, the Wright Brothers, Timothy Barners Lee etc. These people have attained riches and social recognition.

The last category is success resulting from attainment of good result. People in this group may not have lots of money,nevertheless, have got good result in their field. Here we have the academicians (professors), Prof. Uriel W Ayonoadu, Peter F Drucker. The inventors and the scientists like: Thomas Edison, the Wright Brothers, Timothy Barners Lee, our Lord Jesus Christ, boxing champions, football stars, athletes, artists etc.

There are no clear-cut distinction among the people in the various classes because achievement that qualifies somebody in a class has an overlapping appearance on the the other classes; for instance, a stupendously rich person automatically has social recognition, and a re-known inventor or scientist, on the other hand makes a lot of money from his inventions and eventually qualifies as rich; most celebrities are rich, so attempting to strictly classify person in a category of success is a herculin task and may lead to frustration. This is why you may see a person's name in two or more categories- they are interwoven.

The starting point on a journey to success of whatever kind is an aim or a goal. (The direction and the driving force).

Nobody achieves what he or she doesn't aim or set as a goal. Any materialization that doesn't come after aim or goal set is a "luck" and cannot be celebrated as success or achievement; success usually follows aim or objective and comes with joy resulting from accomplishment.

It is pertinent to state here that the focus of this work on success and its principles revolves around these categories of success, therefore, most examples and citations from sources point to success Icons that fit into these classes. This is not to say however, that successes made outside these classes are worthless; no, but as a book, like any other communication medium must have clear perspective and target audience-and again, success in these classes come mainly from setting goals and taking specific actions in accordance with proven principles and knowledge.

A person who succeeds in training his children in a particular way, for instance; in the fear of God and respect for the elderly, first of all, sets "The fear of God and respect for the elderly" as his goal for children's training. He can as well set goals on inculcating negative values and vices, and if the children became violent and criminally minded, he would have also succeeded in that regard.

Similarly, the person who wants riches or high social status, must first set "riches or high social status" as aim, and if he achieves, he would then be considered a success.

Success is a general and loose concept. To be meaningful and appreciated it must be defined in relative term; it must be relative to specific field or activity.

The millionaires and billionaires succeeded in achieving their objectives of being wealthy financially. The social class, rulers, celebrities, musicians, footballers, actors and actresses succeeded in achieving their aim of getting high social recognition. The inventors, scientists, philanthropists succeeded in achieving fame by their contributions and indelible marks on lives of people, making it impossible to not recognize them when we are beneficiaries of their performance and witty inventions. Therefore, success must speak for itself by evidence of the achievement before people's eyes. Nobody's success could be covered, at least for long; it must radiate for all to see.

Success is not for the lazy or indolent, therefore, success seeker must convert their desire for success into actions that will make success possible. This is a hard truth that we must live with;therefore shouldbe prepared to roll up our sleeves for success which we so desire. But how do we achieve this? It is through:

1. Aim
2. Plan
3. Focus and resilience; predicated on knowledge, and actions.

Now, where do we get knowledge? Books, including the one you are reading now, personal interviews and observations, mentors, and personal experience, school and training of course!

To be successful, we must first have the desire and the craving for it; this would propel us to finding the principles.

It is my pleasure to announce to you that reading this book is a demonstration of "desire for success", which is a basic step to success – success is waiting for you!

THE FOUNDATION FOR SUCCESS

I consider four factors as foundation for success; they are (1) Knowledge of yourself i.e your make up (self-discovery). (2) Knowledge of your field or trade. (3) Designing and implementing a purposeful program for realization of goal. (4) Resilience.

Knowledge is a key resource in attaining success; knowledge of yourself and of the field or industry you are or want to go into. It is therefore, an effective approach after having desire for success, to examine your makeup: nature -What you are made up of or called to do. In this area self-study and self-examination is very necessary; this you have to discover by yourself. Nobody else knows you the way you do yourself so, you have to find out; luckily there are plethora ofself-discovery books; may be is apt to introduce you to thefour basic temperaments as identified by Hippocrates: sanguine; the out-going and empathic, extroverted personality; choleric: the active, decisive and extroverted nature; melancholy: the analytical, self-sacrificial, talented, perfectionist and introverted personality; and phlegmatic: the quiet, easy-going and introverted personality.

For and in-depth information on temperament, I introduce you to Tim Lahaye's book: *Why you Act the Way you do*. Hopefully it will help you find the temperament or combination of temperaments that helps you discover your talents. With such discovery, you can align your strength to career that emphasizes your strength for success. A good psychologist can also be of great assistance. Temperament test could be helpful if the skills needed by your field are subtle. Knowledge of yourself will make your success more probable as it will save wasted years of "trial and error", and dissipating energy and resources. For instance it may be an effort in futility for polio-infested person to insist on becoming a boxer or a bricklayer. In the same vein, it will take the grace of God for a person who stammers to make a good carrier in delivering seminar or making public speech, but nevertheless such person can write good and inspiring books. If somebody is only good in talking; he should just ensure he talks wisely and informatively, and then endeavor to connect to those who are fascinated by his wise and informative talk, and they could be his customers; ready to pay for his ability: talk.

Some don't attain success because they can't discover their talent; maybe are not perceptive or discipline enough to find.

Next, is to find knowledge that is basic to success in your chosen field.

All successful people have good knowledge of their field, or know how to employ the services of those who are knowledgeable in their field. Every success points to doing something well; nobody can do well in something he/she doesn't have good knowledge of. So to be successful in any field you must first seek knowledge or seek the service of the one who knows. You tap into the experience and knowledge of those that are ahead of you in your field by reading their books, and attending their seminars.

The Advance Learner's Oxford Dictionary defines knowledge thus:"The information, understanding and skill you gain through education or experience."It also defines "information" as: facts or details about something or somebody."From the above definition, you can deduce that knowledge must come from education, training or experience. And a knowledgeable person in any field is the person who doesn't just have abundance of information on the subject, but also good understanding of it; giving him ability to maneuver the abundant information (data) at his disposal to the achievement of desired goal or result- he should be able to control, direct and deploy it for effective result. This means a knowledgeable person must know or at least anticipate where and when in the organization he works, or in the society (market), if a free-lance, his knowledge is needed. He has the responsibility of making his knowledge productive; otherwise he is as good as the uninitiated.

I strongly believe this gap is the reason why some

academicians are not successful in the financially rich sense of it.

A "knowledge worker," to use Ducker's coined term, for instance: Lawyer, Doctor or Chef must have considerable understanding and skill to effectively use his resource: knowledge, otherwise it becomes useless, if not destructive.

A Chef, for instance should know how to use his ingredients: water, oil (vegetable or palm) fish, and meat (fresh or dried) onions, vegetable… and spices in a definite order to achieve nutritious and tasty meal.

He should first know what kind of meal he wants to cook, how many people he is cooking for and sometimes, whom. He has to think through these questions before lighting his gas cooker; he has to start with the receiver of his service in mind, the customer; with definite result in mind: serving nutritious and tasty meal.

To achieve his goal, he has to decide whether to start with water or oil, whether with vegetable or palm oil, he has to decide on the definite order; even with the order decided, would still decide on the interval between ingredients.

All these he has to skillfully consider and apply, if he must get his desired result. He can't afford to randomly add ingredients like the inexperienced cook, and expect the desired result. Knowing the recipient of the service is particularly important in one sense: tailoring service to suit the specific need and condition of the end-user (customer).This last point can dramatically increase the value of the service to the end-user, which can create loyalty and more money. For instance: a hypertensive person doesn't need much salt; and an ulcer person too doesn't need much pepper- in fact, he will love his chef more if he didn't add pepper at all.

In like mariner an attorney should be able to use his wealth of information and experience to decide which case cited, given the specific situation of the case, will strike the judge as most appropriate and convincing to win the case, get acquittal, or at least reduce the severity of the offence. If a lawyer doesn't have this skill and sense of judgment, he is, in effect, a bad one; he should not be hired. It doesn't matter, which school he graduated, or the size of his library. This same instance could be given of doctors and other knowledge persons, but I think the point has been made. Knowledge is not for its own sake, but for performance; without performance it is useless. In this regard Drucker says "For business success, knowledge must first be meaningful to the customer in terms of satisfaction and value. Knowledge per se is useless; it is only effective through the contribution it makes…. - to customer, markets and end-users". In similar vein, Napoleon Hill in Think and Grow Rich contended that knowledge is not power; "knowledge is only potential power, it becomes power only when, and if it's organized into definite plans of action and directed to definite end." Warren Buffet, the CEO of Barkshere Harthaway, the second richest man as I write, has vast knowledge and skill of the investment world- capital market and fund management. His knowledge in this field is the reason why he has consistently maintained top position in world billionaire ranking. Many stock brokers and fund managers watch Buffet closely for their decision to buy or sell: if he buys, they buy: if he sells, they sell.

Here in Nigeria, the list starts with Aliko Dangote; chairman and owner of the Dangote group, foremost businessman and the current richest black and the 51th in the world; Bishop David Oyedepo, founder and president of the Living Faith Church Worldwide Inc; Pastor Matthew Ashimolowo, founder and president of KICC; These people also demonstrate good knowledge of what they have chosen to do, and as a result are doing very well in their various calling.

Undermining these effective starting points has been the bane of some people's success.

Next is to design and implement a purposeful program

for the realization of goal. Success is the reward for diligent implementation of purposeful program for achievement of goal or set of goals therefore, its program has to be object–focus; resulting from strong desire and resolution to succeed; anything short of this will not amount to success. Anybody who doesn't know this truth about success is likely to find success very evasive as he or she may try his or her hands on every field or career, with exception to his/her calling or talent; this would not allow such person to be discipline and patient to the fruition of his/her efforts.

What about the success story of Michael Jordan, the world renowned baseball player. When he was dropped from his high school baseball team, he through determination to succeed, committed himself to a rigorous, more challenging regime of exercise aimed at re-enlisting himself in the team, his commitment to practice made him become even better than most of his teammates who were not dropped. His success in achieving this goal revealed to him his hidden ability to succeed at whatever objective he set reasonably and pursues: this is not exclusive to him alone; it is widely applicable to almost all.

And finally, resilience; resilience is very necessary for success of any body in any field because success doesn't always come at first attempt, so people seeking for success must have the ability to live above the challenges and obstacles oflife; putting themselves back in order after a great disappointment and adversity

Resource of whatever form: time, money, knowledge, friends, and family has to be deployed and concentrated on accomplishment and of specific desired objective, not to be dissipated on every field that attracts attention.

Some wouldn't believe that "friends & family" are resources, but that is what they are. The Advance Learner's Dictionary defines resource as: "Something that can be used to help achieve an aim." When it comes to making success, friends and family are two critical resources always over looked. Many do not know that their friends and family can make or mare their success at any endeavor, that is why successful people always inform and seek the support of family and friends; they know the truth that nobody succeeds alone. A popular saying goes like this: "behind every successful man is a woman".

discovering your talent and passion early in your journey for success is an advantage you can take on your stride.

Success could be summarized as series of related, correct decisions on your way to a particular place or destination (Goal), therefore in your journey to success, you will make many decisions concerning the correct use of time, money, of friends to keep, other relations, good personality, perseverance and even what to be passionate about; if you must succeed.

"There are no such thing as self-made man, I have had much help and have found that if you are willing to work, many people are willing to help you". O.Wayne Rollins.

In light of the above quoted context, disagree with the person who claims to be "a self-made man". Maybe the he might had overworked himself to the point of forgetting or undermining helps from friends and relations at various times; both in near and distant past. I advise that success-finders should disagree with this myth of "self-made person" 0r be deceived into trying to succeed alone which may end in futility or would take more than the required resources to succeed.

It doesn't make sense to me if a person would insist on re-inventing the wheel or doing it alone when many people have gone through the same road to success before him/her, and are willing to give assistance with little or no cost. Sometimes all that is needed to access help is "ask"

Chapter Two

CAN YOU IDENTIFY SUCCESS EVEN THOUGH FAR-OFF?

If you are given the task of finding somebody you have never seen before, how would you feel about your task- boring and frustrating, right?

Now, consider another scenario in which an onlooker, being aware of your frustration at your boring task, walk up to you with the description of the person you are asked to look for, how would you feel this time?- I guess, relieved and better!

In the second scenario, the person who gave you the description of the person had made your task a lot easier, in like manner; I will make your task of becoming a success easier according to the best of my ability in the field of success by the grace of God.

First, know that opportunity for success is not always obvious to our senses as opportunity; often times it's disguised in form of challenge or threat; it takes keen perception to unravel and exploit.

An instance is how the Swiss lost her market leadership position to the Japanese (The Swiss bitter experience). Switzerland was known world-wide for its expertise and excellence in watch making. This excellence gave her market dominance for over six to seven decades; they were the best in every component of mechanical watch: bearings, mainsprings, gears etc.

Because of their continuous research, they were leading the way in watch innovation: from minute hand, to second hand, to self-winding, to water resistant watches-infact, Swiss watches were synonymous with quality and accurate watches.

But something profound happened between 1967-1980: Swiss researcher found a shift in watch-making from the mechanical, which their excellence and strength lie, to electronic quartz.

To the Swiss, no better watch can be made without the mechanical components. In other words: electronic quartz watch can never supplant mechanical, so when their researcher presented the idea and the model, Swiss watch makers flung the idea as probably too radical and too divorced from the norm. Because they rejected it as irrelevant, showcased their seemingly worthless model (Their hidden opportunity and success) in an exhibition, and the Japanese quickly recognized the opportunity for success, went to their factory with the model, and that was all that led to the deposition of Switzerland from her highly exalted position by the Japanese. The Swiss fell from grace of 65% market share of the world market; the Japanese climb to grace from 1% to 33% of the world market share!

Another instance was a small business in the 70s-the verge of introduction of the personal computer (P.C.)

As the story goes: a small business owner had prior to the wake of PC popularity in the early 80s decided to go into documentation, typing and typist training so rented a space, equipped it with manual type writers and every necessary resource to launch its business.

Meanwhile, a leading computer company was working on the finishing touches on her personal computer to be launched.

In 1981 when the PC was introduced to the market, the producer during its product awareness and marketing campaign, invited the business community and the general public to a trade show and this owner of the typing pool was equally present in the trade show where the computer manufacturer unveiled their PC and extolled the capacity and functionality of the pc. He also highlighted the numerous potential opportunities this invention would present to people who care to seize the opportunity to develop their businesses even to becoming astoundingly rich, the person went on by saying "This is a new dawn for typing, documentation and information technology (ITC)....but at the same time marks the end of an existing method of information handling...."

To every perceptive attendee, this is a prophetic revelation into the future and the world of business: it's like snapping them into the future to peek at it and later returned to the present, giving them the opportunity to be equipped for success when the future becomes the present.

But surprisingly this typing pool owner did not see this obvious success staring at him, so he ignored this opportunity because he rather saw it as threat to the huge investment in his 'dear but obsolete' typing pool.

Infact he rebuked a perceptive friend of his who suggested he change his manual type-writers to PCs saying, "How could you possibly suggest that I should abandon my new business with so much unrecovered cost?"

His argument was that a business cannot make a 'u turn' when it has not recovered cost of investment, so he tried to justify wrong economic argument by clinging and remaining with the past alone with his business and investment while in reality, the world and his customers have moved on to the future-he practically unwittingly shut his business off from his customers, and this ultimately killed his business.

The flaw in the action is trying to recover unrecoverable past cost (Sunk cost), trying to impose yesterday's reality on a changed today.

This mistake is a catastrophe in itself: it doesn't matter how much has been sunk, if the idea is wrong , or the present made it wrong, as the case with many decisions, then the most rational action is to cut the loss and move in another direction, not forcing the past to conform with the present.

This mistake, many trained business people including cost accountants too do.

In the two instances cited, the companies didn't see and accepted the change as an opportunity, but rather as threat: the former, as a threat to their knowledge and expertise, the latter as threat to their investment. They could not recognize opportunity from far.

Sometimes, one single break-through idea is all you need to be astoundingly rich, for example: Tim Barners Lee. You can as well buy the right to somebody else's ingenious or creative ideas with well-written agreement: Bill Gates is a perfect example. He bought the exclusive right to two young men's ingenuity for writing Disk Operation System (DOS).

This singular deal launched him into wealthy places and

world fame. I am sure you might have not heard of names of the writers of this program, yet the smallest boy in your neighborhood certainly had heard of Bill Gates.

Jeff Bezos story to Amazon is similar: reading through an article while in Wall Street, Jeff caught a perception which he swiftly acted on; sold his house, relocated to New Seattle, and was on his way to create Amazon.com, the biggest and most popular online book store. May be you are aware that he employed some computer nerds to help him develop to reality what was hitherto seen by only him, but I am sure you might have not heard of names of the guys that assisted him to make that vision physical.

Second, dispel now, and always the wide-spread belief and the saying 'opportunity comes but once." Opportunity comes always, and it's everywhere! I am convinced that even as you read, there is at least one, or by the time you finish reading, you would be open to some opportunities that have been with you all-week-long which you didn't recognize them as such; you only need to open your senses to, and be more perceptive.

Third, don't always expect opportunity to be obvious. Some of us could not see opportunity until somebody else opens it to our eyes. Often times opportunity comes disguised as problems or challenges that is why some more discerning and positive-minded people rather call it "challenges", and challenges is what brings the best in us; if we confront and win, then we become grateful to ourselves for daring, and also increase our self-confidence and self-esteem, which is necessary for success. If we detest challenges, we may be passing over opportunities, and in this regard Iyanla Vanzant says this: "Challenges come so we can grow and be prepared for things we are not equipped to handle now. When we face our challenges with faith, prepare to learn, willing to make changes, and if necessary, let go, we are demanding our power to be turned on."

To access anything, you must first be aware of its presence; it is your conviction of its availability that will compel and energize you to detailed and pain-staking search that ultimately results to being found. To further prove the above assertion, I bring to you the story of R.U Darby and his uncle: R.U Darby's uncle of Williamsburg, Maryland, during the 'gold fever' days, in his quest to mine gold and become rich, went for a goldmine and began digging for gold, after a week of intense search, discovered some shiny ore materials but needed machinery to extract it so he went home and mobilized the machinery and R.U Darby, then continue the mine, they mined with increasing hope until the vein of gold disappeared , and they quit and sold away the machinery to a Junkman: end of search.

The junkman employed the service of a mine engineer,

the engineer calculated the fault line and said that gold would be found three feet from where Darby's uncle stopped, and he was right- three feet, gold was indeed found. One obvious lesson we can deduce from this story is that neither R.U Darby nor his uncle had the conviction that gold actually existed in that particular mine, so the rational thing to do, after some unsuccessful attempts was to quit and either go elsewhere for next search or give up the search altogether.

In contrast, the engineer through his experience, expertise and calculation was sure that gold existed.

Let us picture same issue in a more revealing scenario in which we might had found ourselves: you misplaced something in a room which only you have the key and consequently use or enter. You are convinced that this missing object could only be in the room in which only you have access, and the last time you used the missing object was in the room, and could not recall when you took it outside. With that conviction, you restricted your search to that room until you eventually found. No amount of persuasion would have compelled you to search elsewhere.

Fourth, don't believe that success is only resident in far or foreign country. This belief too, like the absence of knowledge and conviction, have kept many people from success: they believe that until they travel abroad for greener pasture, they can't make it, and they reserve all connections and network till when they are granted visa; if they didn't get the visa, they wait endlessly and die a failure.

The story was told of Ali Hafed in Conwel's *Acres of Diamond* who shared same belief. Hafed was a prosperous farmer, but in his erroneous belief that success (Riches) dwells only in far-away or foreign country, sold and deserted his fruitful farm in search for great wealth in mythical diamond fields. He wandered and roamed all the rest of his life to no avail searching for wealth everywhere but his back yard, and eventually died a pauper. Shortly after his death, expensive quality of diamond was reported being found- right in Ali Hafed's sold land! This story validates a popular Yoruba adage: "what you are looking for in Sokoto is in your shokoto".

Though this story dated decades ago, its' relevance to our time cannot be questioned because many are still like Ali Hafed, believing they can only make it if they leave the shore of their country, but it is not true.

I hope the story debunks the misconception that claims that until people travel abroad, they could not be successful.

The following successful persons make their wealth and fame residing in their country.

(1) Mr. Aliko Dangote   -   Nigeria

(2) Bishop David Oyedipo-   Nigeria

(3) Pst. David Ibeomeye   -   Nigeria

(4) Linda Ikeji   -   Nigeria

(5) Tuface   -   Nigeria

(6) Mr. Macmillan Woha -   Nigeria

If gaining visa guarantees success, then how come many Nigerians are languishing abroad; with thick-dark-veil of shame and frustration covering their self-esteem and confidence? They find it difficult to bear the reality that those friends whom they left at home are now their better. The same is true of some foreigners who are languishing and dying as paupers in Nigeria; this is self evident and does not need supporting with names

I herefore challenge you to perish such thought; if at all you share in it. Look inward and around for opportunities; find out what you should know, who you need to associate with, what new skill you should learn to complement and make your present skill(s) saleable, then receive your "breakthrough"! Success in any field is not much about what is outside but inside, not much about what you don't have but about the little you have. No wonder God in his infinite wisdom admonishes us not to despise the days of little beginning. Zechariah 4:10.

Fifth, know that success doesn't have a fixed identity. This could be a painful truth about success, yet we must know that success doesn't have a fixed identity or residence (address); maybe, that is why it comes and goes- easily, if not perpetuated.

It is a known secrete of success that it is shy, and would want to be wooed just like a woman; probably that is why it doesn't come early. It would elude us many times, keeping us waiting and expecting, wanting to try our patience and love for it; whether we will be willing to wait, no matter how long; whether we are prepared to pay the price, not minding how much.

Even when it finally showed up, it may come from different way: door, window or even back-door; this is why some are still expecting it from front door, on a particular form, it had sneak in through back door in different form- properly disguised, such that we may not recognize!

It surprises me what many people, especially youths can give in sacrifice to win approval and appearance of that girl they are wooing in their houses: they may stay long awake, make midnights calls, wait patiently on promise upon promises, make all needed sacrifices, humble themselves where humility is needed, map out plans and strategies that will amaze you of their ingenuity and patience.

These persons caught in this frenzy may be ready to pay any price, even unto death!

These people unleash their innate abilities and talents

just to get approval of an opposite sex in relationship. Many inmates are in prison because of trying to woo the love of sex partner. You might have had of Richard Robles who claimed he wanted to abstain from crime after being paroled in August 1963 for three-year sentence but still robbed Janice and Emiley, and eventually killed them to provide for his girlfriend and his three-year old sister, "both of them desperately needed money", he said. As Goleman revealed in his *"Emotional Intelligence"*, this killing kept him in prison for more than 30 years! But tell half of those inmates to rather channel half the effort or risk they took that sent them to jail for success, they won't agree; they would lose patience and ability.

The level of sacrifice you are prepared to make to get something signifies the importance of that thing to you. Your beliefs determine your actions, knowingly or unknowingly.

Indeed success doesn't have a fixed identity that is why anybody who has conditioned his or her mind to believe that success must come in a definite form is likely to continue searching while in effect, it has come. The nature and appearance of my success would be different from yours; even to the same individual, area of success in one field is different from another. Knowing these truths about success is like revealing its nature, and will alert your senses to recognize it when you are searching.

If you know that what you are searching for is not easily recognizable even when it has come, this knowledge will not let you limit your search to few areas that may not even possess, but be more general, sensitive and perceptive while searching.

Often times, as earlier said, success comes in forms that you least expected; in form of challenges, in helping hand responding to desperate need, charity, passion to end an anomaly or in mundane assignment from friend or boss, Jeff Bezos is a typical example.

Our thought is basic to what we become; no wonder the Bible says *"As a man thinketh in his heart so is he"* (quotation).

Another passage admonishes us to guide our heart with all diligence out of it are the issues of life. Prov. 4:23.

Also consider this philosophical truth: *"If you think you are beaten, you are, if you dare not, you don't. if you like to win but think you can't it is almost certain you won't."*

In summary, I advise that while you want success; be open minded; don't confine your search to a particular source, because it is fond of coming from wherever it likes. In addition, be kind and friendly because people rarely succeed alone; you need the support of people of different calibers; they will be willing to assist you only if they see you worthy of their assistance: and that is a function of your personality, relationship, and charisma. If people hardly succeed alone, then it follows that you should be humble yet courageous enough to ask for help when necessary. It could save you sweat and delayed success.

Many don't achieve success because are too proud to ask for help, or are full of negativism and self-doubt resulting from low self esteem which denies or delays success.

If you are holding down your success because of fear of rejection; will it please you to know that many are willing to share their knowledge with others because it gives joy when they teach, and in the process know more; it is an irony of teaching that the person who teaches get to know better than he or she would have known, if he/she didn't teach somebody.

So go ahead and ask for help whenever necessary, you may by not asking for help you are inadvertently backpedaling your success. In case you ask and was refused, take solace in the fact that the refusal doesn't change your name or in any way limit you; it could be that you haven't yet meet the right person, or the person was not in the right frame of mind as at when you asked; if you persist, you will definitely win.

However, sometimes all that is needed to turn "No" to "yes" is a little token (cash), remember, 'what you are willing to sacrifice to get something signifies its importance to you.' Remember, *there is no such thing as something for nothing*"!

I have said in previous paragraph that often time success comes disguised in mundane activities or tasks, yet it worth repetition here. I therefore introduce you to the story of Mr. Barnes and the American great inventor: Mr. Thomas Edison. Mr. Edward Barnes in search for success wanted to partner with the American great inventor in the 20th century, Mr. Thomas Edison; with determination, Barnes found his way through and into Orange, New Jersey to seek partnership with Edison.

On reaching Edison's office, Barnes introduced himself and his mission of working as an associate with Edison. He was not offered his desired position at start, but accepted and work happily on some menial job that was given to him, for very nominal wages. The job assignment, apparently was not important to Edison, but Barnes knew that as long as he works within Edison's organization, there is the possibility to showcase his abilities that would endear him to his dream associate (Edison) which eventually will make him succeed on his goal: *"A man's gift maketh room for him, and bringgeth him before great men"* Prov. 18:16 (KJV). Though, Barnes didn't know how and when, but he was certain that it will happen someday, and finally it did when the opportunity showed up in Edison's new invention and office device called "The Ediphone", which did not appeal to Edison's sale men; they felt it will take a great effort to sell.

However, Barnes saw his disguised opportunity in this new device and promised to market it, and he did marvelously well that Edison signed a contract with him to distribute it nationwide. Thus made him "A sole distributor" With the signing of this marketing contract, Barnes has achieved his goal of becoming Edison's associate.

The opportunity though, was hidden in a contrivance which interests no one but Barnes, and of course the inventor (Edison), Barnes did recognize his opportunity, and challenge himself to market it successfully: he was able to recognize success from far. The question is, can you too recognize success or opportunity from far?

Chapter Three

VISION AND GOAL

Vision and goal are so essential for success of any kind and field that they deserve a chapter dedicated to them.

Vision, according to the Advanced Learner's English Dictionary: *"The ability to think about or plan the future with great imagination and intelligence"*. The Holy Bible says in Proverbs 29:18 that "Where there is no vision, the people perish". Meaning; if a person doesn't have vision, (s)helives a wayward life, so cannot accomplish any worthy achievement, and this is very true.

Goal, according to Dr. David Schwatz: *"Goals are essential to success as air is to life."* Vision and goal are closely related, so are often used interchangeably: vision is the entirety of desired future actualization while goal is a definite aim that actions are directed at, for realization. When group of goals related to vision are achieved, the vision would have been achieved. Goals are stepping stones to vision. Many re-known success and management writers have stressed the important of vision and goal to success.

Brian Tracy, an American famous public speaker and

best seller author, in his book: ***Goal!***, says "Your ability to set goal is the master skill of success" in other words he is reiterating the relevance of goal in success pursuit hence I paraphrase his statement thus: every successful person has mastered the skill of goal setting, so if you want to become successful in any field, then you must learn how to set, and of cause achieve goal. Some success seeker don't take the issue of goal setting seriously; maybe that is why they fail, they feel it is time-consuming and therefore a waste of time so, should be avoided. Some recognize the position of goal in success attainment but don't know how to set it.

Goal has an undeniable position in the scheme of success. Time spent on setting goal is never wasted, rather it speeds up, and increase the possibility of success as it makes easier for you to focus on the important things; the various activities or programs which must be done to succeed.

When goals is set concerning any pursuit, the person clearly knows what he wants to succeed at; and therefore identify the critical activity or activities he must forge ahead with inorder to succeed; he wouldn't scatter resources on competing alternatives, or on less important things to the detriment of the goal- activities are planned and prioritized.

Goal, especially when written provides you with clear picture, if clearly defined. It helps you know what you should involve your resources in. it also keeps you reminded, and reaffirms your result along the way to success, avoiding detour.

To prove the importance of goal, and in writing to success, I bring to you a research conducted of the graduating students of the Harvard Business School between 1979 and 1989. The purpose was to prove the importance of goal setting to success in whatever field. The story goes: graduating MBA students of Harvard Business School were asked in 1979 "how many of you have set a clearly, written goal to accomplish in the future?" It was revealed that only three percent (3%) had clear written goals, while thirteen percent (135) had set goals, but not on paper (it was on their minds) and the remaining eighty four percent (84%) had no goals! Ten years later-1989, the students were interviewed again to see the impact of goals on their achievements; their results were true reflection of the level of their preparedness for success: the three percent who had clearly written goals was earning on average about ten times more than the ninety seven percent (135)(put together) who had goals but only in mind was on average, twice better (in terms of income then eighty four (84%) who did not have goals was poor; some of this eighty four percent were derelicts so to speak!

I hope this story which could be verified from other related books will urge you to be discipline enough to write down your goals because the top three percent is where you belong!.

When setting goals, there is a profound technique that has evolved, and it is represented by the acronym-SMART. SMART is an acronym for the following words with brief explanation.

"S" stands for specific: goals should be clearly specified, in an unambiguous statement; else it becomes source of confusion for anybody using it as a guide.

"M" stands for measurable: goals should be measureable. In attempt to measure anything, unit of measurement must be applied to make it effective and monitor progress as the plans are being executed. Expressing goals in a quantitative terms, or even qualitative terms for goals that bother on "value" is a very good step to make achievement of goal possible.

"A" stands for align to major goal. On the road to success of any goal, are many other goals of different levels of importance; dimensions and requirements, time frame and implementation strategy, and so forth. With many goals before you, it is very easy for a goal's interest and purpose to conflict with one another; thereby making your efforts counter-productive and resource wasting. Solution: align all goals to major goal- make all goals complementary, not competing.

"R" stands for realistic: goal should be and should have sufficient evidence of the reality on ground, not fantasy or 'blind faith': many of us are guilty of this while making plans. We often think that sheer wish, good intention or even faith would do but often times, they don't. I know many religious people will vehemently disagree with this; let me prove.

A growing church with about two hundred adults

which I was a member wanted to celebrate her pastor's birthday with a generous gift of life-time: a stately home. Following the decision to buy him a property, a committee was set to source befitting property, and report to the church; it decided on a forty million naira (40,000,000) house with sound-proof power generator, and lots of goodies.

To raise the money, it (the committee) brought the proposal and photograph of the glamorous house for everybody to see and contribute toward. In one of the fund-raising meetings, considering our relatively small size, and inability to raise one million five hundred thousand naira (N1.5m) for a failed interlocking project of our premises for a almost a year, I was quick to object to the new project, even though such property would have speak volume of love for our beloved daddy. I opposed the project in one of those fund raising meetings, suggesting that a cheaper project or gift should be bought instead, pointing out that "faith" and "finance" are two different areas. I was censured and called a "faithkiller". As the birthday draws nearer, the reality of our financial ability, and the relevance of my objection began to sink in: They started adjusting the value of the gift till finally settled on an un-developed plot of land, in a less developed area- yet with bargain on installment payment. Such is what happens when the reality on ground is ignored in setting goal!

Another instance of 'not considering the reality' in goal

(project) would have been demonstrated by me but was corrected before it was too late. The story goes: in the year 2013 when I wanted to build my first house in Port Harcourt. With overzealousness, and sheer determination, I wanted a one-storey building with three bedrooms down, and two standard bedrooms up. I hurriedly engage an architect to draw plan, and he did a nice job.

With the fine plan on my hands, before I began, it occurred to me to hear from the architect about an estimated cost for the project When he told me the minimum cost, that was when I knew that. building a storey building that my family can live safely in without fear of possible collapse and its inherent trauma and loss, cannot be compared to just a bungalow!

At the end of the meeting with my architect, I tossed the plan far away and headed for a simple but standard two bedrooms flat, and another three self contained apartment at the front of the two bedroom. With this adjustment, it still took me about a year to finish everything about the two bedrooms, and move in.

As I write, the three self-contained is still at window seat level, but I have moved in on the flat! Thanks to applying the principle of reality on ground to my goal of building my first house in Port Harcourt. Often times I see people build a storey building (As if it were a condominium) for seven to ten years! Needless to say, if such person have integrated the reality, and adjusted his plan, he could complete his project earlier and move in and benefit from his house-may be such person doesn't know that building house is like a capital project, in which there are little or no benefit derivable from the project unless it is completed: money spent from the beginning till any uncompleted point is like a locked money kept idle for the entire period.

Finally, "T" which stands for time bound. Every goal should have a time frame- an expected accomplishment time. Without the urgency of time frame, we may never get started, or be serious; no wonder Peter Ferdinand Drucker said "work without deadline is not work assigned but work toyed with"

Chapter Four

LET YOUR DREAMS DRIVE YOU TO SUCCESS

Often times I meet people who say they have dreams but act in manner that is inimical to the realization of their dreams- they don't let their dreams drive them. Those who merely parrot their dreams, and then expect their fruition probably thought that having or at best parroting dreams is all they need to actualize and become successful; nothing could be farther from the truth than this misconception.

All successful people around the globe let their dreams drive them. They live their dreams- so to speak. Thomas Edison let his dream drove him as was demonstrated in his action to leave his newly wedded wife at home barely an hour after their wedding ceremony, and went straight to the factory to perform those never-ending experiments- worse still, he was so immersed in his experiments that couldn't recall that that was his wedding day and they were supposed to be on honey moon rather, he stayed all through the rest of the day,and late into the night until his friend exclaimed

"Tom, what are you doing at this late hour?". "What time is it? Edison astonishingly asked.

"Midnight!" the friend responded.

"Midnight?" he asked rhetorically "is that so?" I must go home then, I was married today".

Only inclination to live his dreams can make a newly wedded groom consider the seemingly insane thought of leaving his bride lonely at home on a wedding day, and rather be romancing with wires, metals and experiments. Edison did not only think of it, he did. Something many people wouldn't dare to do-and could you believe it was on Christmas day, when virtually everybody is on holiday!

Maybe you should turn to the Bijanis' story for better conviction. As the story was clearly told by Dr. Ben Carson in his *Take the Risk*. Fortunately and maybe coincidentally too Dr. Carson, the author was among the 28 physicians and over 125-member-medical team that separated the 29 yr.- old Iranian conjoined twin sisters, Ladan and Lelah Bijani- both lawyers.

Ladan and Lelah were 29 years Conjoined twins whom for the craving for living their dream of separate lives drove them, and even unto death, dare the uncharted water.

These twin sisters have lived lives all through birth (infancy) to adulthood at 29 yrs.. Together they lived as one indivisible but with separate and distinct personalities, forging ahead with living and taking unanimous decision on virtually all matters even to their dislike till their last day. They desperately wanted to live normal, individual, and distinctly different lives.

Despite medical expert advice against the operation because of its low probability of success, the Bijanis defiantly insisted it should be done. Dr. Carson noted that a group of German doctors had deemed the operation "too dangerous".

Dr. Carson, a renowned neurologist made this frantic effort to dissuade them based on his experience, expertise and the report before him. This was what he told them "Based on my experience and my study of your case, and despite the excellent resources available to your fine surgical team here at Raffles Hospital, I still think there is at least a 50 percent chance this operation could result in death or serious damage for one or both of you. I need to make certain you both understand that".

But they assured Ben that they were fully aware of the risk involved; as that has been drummed in their ears enough times by every honest and well-meaning person.

However, this was their determined reply: "We would

rather die than not pursue this if there is any chance we could be free to live our own separate lives. Death would be better than continuing to live like this".

Unfortunately they died. They believed in the success truth of letting their dream drive them- to the Bijanis, individuality was much a dream to their heart as riches and fame are to some of us.

Now consider another instance of being driven by dream. Mr. George Lucas, the moviemaker who produced *Star Wars,* revolutionized the movie industry and made billions of dollars from it. Had the dream of being an independent moviemaker; that took him to film school to prepare for the actualization of his dream. His father rather wanted him to join the family retail business but to George, that would not lead to fulfillment of his dream and realization of joy, so he was rather committed to his dream. When things were rough financially, yet he needed to finance a movie, he got loan from his father, and with it he made his first breakthrough as he turned student award-winning movie into his first feature film. Then a juicier offer followed to make another movie, but in spite of its attractiveness, he didn't consider it as such. He rather worked on perfecting a movie he believed in, and consequently made success and reap lot of cash from it. He gathered the money from the movie, and also sold his house to finance yet another movie which shot him to lime-light. He says, in his opinion, "Success is not about the money, but about the freedom to follow his dreams and pursue his passion. If he took an easier path and did what everyone else did, or what his father expected him to do- he doubted he would ever be happy…"

JOHN S. MATTHEW

Chapter Five

CAN YOU TURN A STUMBLING BLOCK TO STEPPING STONE?

"Remember, nothing that is good works by itself, just to please you, you have to make the damn thing work." –Thomas Alva Edison.

"Life is not a bed of roses" says a popular adage.

In life, men are to pass through difficulties and challenges at different stages while trying to achieve set goals; some are simple, others are tough to overcome. Having this in mind prepares us ahead of the challenges, so we can make plans to exploit them, avert or build resilience and remain resolute at our pursuit. If a man is resilient, the wise thing to do is to continually evolve new approaches to solution, so he goes back to the challenge each time with new ideas to try.

A problem, limitation or stumbling block is a situation that impedes progress or success of an activity, therefore, to progress, you must solve it. Otherwise you will be blocked for as long as the problem remains.

For instance, a group that you belong is currently facing problem of some sort; to the ordinary person, that is a problem that needs to be detested and avoided, but to the perceptive, imaginative and creative person, it is challenge, and needs to be embraced and confronted.

If any person, whether within or outside the group proffers solution, he must be paid for, except he "wants to act" Father Christmas.

He can definitely name his price; determine his special condition of service.

The more difficult the problem (which probably many people might have tried) the more money and fame he will get-that is, more successful he will become.

Challenge however, is what brings out the best in us; many would not have realized their potentials, if not for challenges that they conquered while following their dreams. As source of encouragement and motivation, I bring to you from the Bible, 1corinthians 10:13: "There hath not temptation taken you but such as is common to man: "but God is faithful, who will not suffer you to be tempted above that you are able, but will with the temptation also make a way to escape, you may be able to bear it". For the above citation to be more relevant to you, I suggest you substitute "temptation" with "challenge", and "bear" with "win". There could be no truer statement than the above Bible quotation when it comes to facing challenges, and winning.

God has endowed us with so much potential that many use an insignificant proportion of it in life-time! To prove this, look around and marvel at the creative and ingenuous ability of menaround the world from days of Adam till today: uncountable discoveries, devices and concept brought forward by people as solutions to challenges of human being. Thomas Edison alone patented more than a thousand inventions!

To help you jettison the cynism that may attribute the success of these men to their color of skin and technological advancement, I tell you of local, yet classical story of turning a stumbling block to ultimate success; leveraging on resilience. Here comes the story: an Idoma young man,Hillary AgboOdeh of Ohimini Community in Benue State of Nigeria. After his secondary education picked up remedial form to study medicine and surgery in the Benue State University, Nigeria, but was rather offered admission to study Physics, although, he was among the best remedial students of that batch.

Reluctantly he accepted the Physics offer; probably for the sake of being admitted into university of his choice. However, accepting the university's choice course came with a price of poor academic performance; performed poorly to the extent of 17 carryover courses when level 300results was released! This poor performance made him subject of mockery by friends and peers, and a subject of probation and waft contemplation by the school authority. The impending waft took him to a 'turning point': when he decided to enroll for Joint Admission and Matriculation Board(JAMB) to study a-medicine-related course: Psychology in which he graduated with astounding performance of 4.57 CGPA (first class) and multiple awards, including: pioneer first class in the Department of Psychology from the university since it was established, the best graduating student of the 14th and 15th combine convocation of the school, and more!

Let us dwell a bit on the success of this young Nigerian who indeed turned a stumbling block to a stepping stone. Obviously this was no mean feat, coincidence or luck as the cynics would classify; this success was based on resilience, and determination to succeed. As said earlier, success doesn't come cheap, and may come in form of challenges and obstacles, only those who are prepared to succeed will ultimately succeed.

Hillary set his goal, pursued it with determination and commitment to succeed even when success doesn't seem possible. He didn't give up, he was resolute about graduating with good grade rather than part of the third class crowd with just poor performance comment on a mere piece of paper bearing the name and the logo of his school, no; he wanted success- an outcome that distinguishes him from the rest. He must have devoted a lot of his time during this period to study rather than to other competing social and leisurely activities (proper resource allocation). He took critical decision not to quit but change direction and approach: write JAMB at final year and began a different course at level

100 with younger ones fresh out of secondary school as freshman in the same university- something many of us would not dare to do. He recognized that decision as being critical and a turning point for him, so he took, not minding what anybody would say. Some of us would not dare to do that which will make us succeed in career simply because of others' opinions and comments- that would be cowardice of us.

When you are on the journey to success, what others say about you is inconsequential provided what you are doing is morally right; do it- they will turn round to praise and dine with you if you succeed. After all, a friend of mine says this parable "tongue has no bone", so it runs to-fro, up-down, that is why it praises and condemns".

Recall that I have said earlier that 'if a man is resilient, the wise thing to do is to continually evolve new approach to solution, so he goes back to the challenge each time with new idea to try-that is exactly what he did when Physics didn't give him a break. An essential ingredient for success is to know when to change direction or approach after many failed attempts- this is the "turning point", but unfortunately, many couldn't recognize this point.

There is a level of joy that comes with every achievement of goal; and the level of joy is proportional to the level of difficulty encountered when pursuing the goal; the joy itself is derived from the difficulty inherent in the goal, the proving out of your ability. Often time we don't fully grasp our ability till we dare to try, and if successful, we become proud and thank God we did.

Needless to say, if these persons were not resolved, resilient, and believed in their God-given abilities, the varieties of devices, machines wouldn't have been available today. Apparently, they didn't quit and complain, were not discouraged by the stumbling blocks of life before them rather, they thought through, brain stormed, consulted, researched, and re-strategized then finally won and reap the fruit there from.

Many are too quick to quit. Some quit at the first sign of challenge as if life were a bed of roses-they discourage themselves, worst of all, some go a bit farther discouraging everybody who attempts to do what they failed at, as if their ability were standard measurement for everyone else's. Stay away from people who discourage you because they tried that same thing and failed! –that they failed does not corroborate your failure.

Those who vow never to try something new, or believe that nobody succeeds at what they failed are not fair to themselves and others- they didn't try the "one more time" that bring success.

Chapter Six

DO YOU KNOW ALIBIS OR ALLIES?

"Some men have thousands of reasons

Why they cannot do what they want

to, when all they need is one reason

they can." Dr. Willis R. Whitney.

"Sir, I have no man, when the water is stirred, to put me into the pool: but while I am coming, another stepped down before me" John 5:7 – excuse. The above is a statement of excuse made to Jesus by the man with thirty eight years of paralysis at the pool of Bethesda. Alibi, a.k.a excuse is in human nature since creation. We generally make excuses to shroud our weaknesses, selfishness, laziness, ill-will, and even to get sympathy from others. In the case of the man with paralysis, he wanted to get Jesus' sympathy with it. No matter how plausible the excuse, it remains an excuse; nothing meaningful can be achieved with it except a temporary relief and comfort.

As long as we focus on excuses, we can never face our

challenges and become successful; every successful man knows this truth and finds solution to problem rather than excusing himself. In facing our problems squarely, we learn more about life and discover our hidden potentials that unlock our success. Many, when faced with challenges, instead of thinking through the challenges for possible solution, spend enormous time and energy to come up with plausible reasons why they would fail, or couldn't try confronting the problem at all.

If we focus on excuses we will see more of our weaknesses than strengths, and will relinquish control of the situation to our weaknesses rather than putting our strengths in charge. If we blame others for our failures, we are in effect saying that others have prerogative to determine our level of success in life, but this we know is pure abdication and is not right. That we have weakness doesn't make us less achievers; everybody has weaknesses and strength. However, some weaknesses are more inhibiting on success in a particular field than the other; we should rather engage our strengths in fields that produce the most result: a comparative advantage scenario. We only limit ourselves by focusing more on, or maybe over-rating the potential of things we don't have so we don't utilize the one we have, or maybe trample on our most potent ability. So long as we keep on relying on, and building on excuses, we will become very smart at it, and at the same time growing our resistance to anything, person that doesn't give in to our excuses; we see them as the real problem and therefore detest them.

If you feel caught in the web of indulging in excuses for your failure, then this book is appropriate for you: *"Think and grow rich"* by a famous American legend, Napoleon Hill. In this success-building classic book, on the chapter "The devil's workshop" the author, Hill listed what he called the 55 famous alibis (excuses). If you go through it, you too may see your favorite excuse as I saw mine then.

When you see them, dissociate yourself from them all-even your favorite should turn your worst enemy because they are the real enemies to your success, not your friends, relations, parents, or uncles as you may think!

GET A DESIRE OR REMAIN A DAY-DREAMER

Lack of desire is another reason people don't succeed. Many pass over success because of lack of desire. Desire is not synonymous with "sheer wish", it is rather backed by strong will. Theron Q Dumont puts it more precisely in his *The Power of Concentration* thus: "Will power is better asset than money; will carry you over chasms of failure, if you give it a chance."In contrast, wish is just ordinary and in abundance- every person has enough of it, and nothing can be achieved with it. Desire has a great potential for achievement and accomplishment of any goal. Desire, especially if intense, has a way of delivering to people plans that if backed with actions, bring the achievement of whatever goal set. Consider the case of intense desire for sex; where people otherwise confused and ineffective suddenly become active, intelligent and articulate; that is how powerful desire can be. The achievement of any goal through the power of desire doesn't need much on the part of the desiring person; just a strong desire couple with belief in your plans and ability, and perseverance to follow your plans through to the day of accomplishment, that is all.

Instances of effectiveness of desire to transmit into reality are too numerous to mention; but it suffices to draw attention to few like: C. Barnes; eventually becoming Thomas Edison's associate after having strong desire, backed with actions and persistence. Marshall Field is another example where his desire to rebuild his store in its original position no matter how many times it got burnt has proven the power of desire-the store remains in his desired position. What about the man who transported his army to fight against an enemy's army whose number was greater than his, yet upon docking on the enemy's shore, burnt the boat that conveyed his armies to the battle; ensuring that they do their best to fight and win or perish because there was no means of going back!

In the few examples above, and many more that you can imagine, desire and belief are inseparable elements that gave them plan(s) and courage to follow their plans through no matter what it takes. Many are so ill-willed and full of inertia that they ended up a day-dreamer.

Majority of this class fail more to lack of desire than anything else. Some think that lack of desire is a sign of humility and holiness- they never know it is a weakness and the comfort of the "none-entity".

Always desire something worthy; it could be just a virtue; desire it and pursue it diligently to achievement. As shown in the beginning of this book, success is not synonymous with wealth alone- it could be in other worthy calling that brings joy to you and people around: remember Mother Theresa.

JOHN S. MATTHEW

Chapter Seven

GET PASSION AND PERSEVERANCE OR FORGET ABOUT SUCCESS

"Nothing in the world cantake the place

ofpersistence. Talent will not: nothing is

more common than unsuccessful men with

talent. Genius will not:....Education will not; the world is full of

educated derelicts. Persistence and

determination alone are omnipotent.

The slogan "press on" has solved and

Always will solve the problems

Ofhuman race".

CALVIN COOLIDGE

Passion and perseverance are other essentials of success in any field. No matter your chosen field, career or calling; success would always elude you without passion and perseverance. May that not be your portion as you develop passion and perseverance. Throughout history, no worthy achievement had ever been made without passion and perseverance. Both home and abroad evidence abound where success is achieved after long trials, and resolution to press on until success is achieved.

Studying biographies of successful people around the globe reveal that success couldn't have been achieved if not for passion and perseverance. Because success doesn't come easy, it is always preceded with heart-rending experiences.

Thomas Alva Edison, the wizard of Menlo Park and arguably the most prolific inventor of the 19th century. Though epitomized passion and perseverance, was confronted with immense adversity of all kinds: from just three months of formal schooling to deafness at the prime age of thirteen; to the utter rejection of his vote recorder by both Massachusetts and Washington legislature; to near eye blindness resulting from testing nickel's suitability for incandescent light; to the mundane task of recording daily experiment and result of his investigations; to the refusal of Western Union to grant him permission to dismantle its office duplex telegraph wiring and battery system, so could enable him test his newly improved duplex of transmitter; to the fiasco of the trial when a rival company, Atlantic and Pacific Telegraph Company encouragingly allowed him dismantle their connection and replace with his own: after many days of repeated failed attempts at successfully testing his improved duplex transmitter, return to Boston to the scornful adversaries of his, who never believed in his abilities – this was egg on his face and reputation!

More travail followed as if he had not seen enough; the misfortune he thought has left at Boston seemed to haunt him to New York: his only friend in New York whom he thought could help with lending some money for food and probably provide him a place to lay his head till he finds job was not at home! He had to roam through the streets the first night in New York. He was like a tramp for some couple of days.

In spite of these misfortunes and many more that life tried to swamp him with, he was able to overcome and became stupendously successful and famous with the help of passion and perseverance.

Without passion for your career, you will be discouraged and give in to failure by every challenge on your way. Without perseverance, he couldn't have put in the decades of trials and errors that the convoluted incandescent light experiments required before his success.

Nothing short of passion and perseverance could keep a person going in face of these, and many more misfortunes and challenges.

Henry Ford, a protégé and dear friend of Thomas Edison worked passionately and tirelessly with his automobile crew before they got their v8 engine.

Abraham Lincoln, the 16th president of America also demonstrated passion and perseverance unto international recognition and success. Lincoln, a man of poor economic background, in the face of stern ill-luck and temporary failure, was able to re-organize himself for several political activities and at several unsuccessful electoral offices elections, finally made it to the much elevated and envious state-manly position of the president of the United States of America.

Back home here in Nigeria, the passion and the perseverance of President Mohamadu Buhari could only be compared to that of his American counterpart: the legendary Abraham Lincoln. Buhari, after serving as military head of states of Nigeria, began his debut political journey to Aso Rock of Nigeria in the year 2003 when he contested as president and failed. With perseverance and resilience, he soon forgot the past and warmed up for another election in 2007 which he also failed. Not deterred by these failures, he patiently waited for another time: 2011, and failed yet another time!

Distraught by the continual failures at his presidential ambition and his commitment to serve his country, he wept, and vowed after the result of 2011 elections were announced, "never to contest again".

Sharing in his grief, animus loyalists were livid, and

went on rampage that killed, and maimed innocent victims; some youth corpers who served as INEC ad-hoc staff were in the list of victims; houses and other properties worth millions of naira were destroyed.

Nothing other than passion to serve his dear country could be responsible for taking him through the incessant failures, yet deciding to contest one more time after his party, Congress for Progressive Change (CPC) formed alliance with two other parties (ANPP and ACN) to form All Progressive Congress (APC). As the result played out at the collation center at the International Conference Center, Abuja. To the surprise of most Nigerians, including me: he won an incumbent president- an unprecedented political milestone in the history of Nigeria!

Michael Jordan became the best base-ball player after he was dropped from his school baseball team for incompetence. These are testimonies of power of passion and perseverance for attainment of success.

The basic qualities that are common among these winners are passion and perseverance. Success doesn't come at first attempt. No! It seems to come after many failed attempts, and this is where passion and perseverance come to the aid of those who have them.

It is natural that we despair and wither away when we fail at an objective however, penalizing and condemning ourselves to the point of not trying again is only self-defeating; because if we fail to try again, then we have failed really.

When people are overwhelmed with failure, they should draw from the qualities of passion and perseverance. They need to know this truth that "failing to try again after failure is the failure itself". It is therefore expedient that they manage to get over failure quickly; put a fresh and rejuvenating look and head on for another try until success ultimately arrives.

Passion is like grease to an engine which helps to avoid friction which consumes energy, and maybe break down of engine at last. The person who is passionate about his goals would always try and re-try. He doesn't give in to discouragement by circumstances around, rather encourages himself, and say 'it doesn't matter how many times I fail, what matters is my ultimate success, and I must not give up till I win'.

Those who have passion and perseverance, are always cheered up by these two ingredients of success the way sports fans do to their team members; they encourage and support till their team win.

A word of caution here! Perseverance doesn't mean being head-strong in the wrong direction. I am sure you have heard of the saying that 'doing the same thing over and over but expecting a different result is insanity of mind"; balance is necessary in everything, and knowing when to change direction or approach after reasonable failed attempts is a confirmation of "true wisdom" – The story of the Idoma genius, Hillary is a classic case of knowing when to change direction, and which direction to go.

What the above caution points out is, while we are

passionate and persevere, we should keep our eyes and other senses alert to the evolution around us because it is these evolutions that judge, validate or invalidate our actions.

We are all witnesses to actions that were once correct and excellent; now turned wrong and appalling to think of – the environments that made them right have gone! Repeating them will never amount to success.

JOHN S. MATTHEW

Chapter Eight

GET EDUCATION –THE BASICS, NOT DEGREES

"I once took an IQ test where the questions seemed absurd. I couldn't focus on any of the mathematical problems, and I think that I scored about zero. I worry about all the people who have been classified as stupid by these kinds of IQ tests. Little do these people know that often these IQ test have been dreamed up by academics who are absolutely useless at dealing with the practicalities of the outside world." – Richard Branson.

The Advanced learner's Dictionary defines Education: "A process of teaching, training and learning, especially in schools or colleges, to improve knowledge and develop skill."

Yes, education is central to success, but not "degrees." This bitter truth needs to be told especially to those who mistakenly think that degree or degrees automatically transmute to success and riches.

If you carefully study the lives of some of the foremost successful and famous people, both of old and present in the world, you will confirm that it doesn't take certificates or degrees but education to be successful in most fields of human endeavor, or even to be astoundingly rich.

Mr. Thomas A. Edison, the great inventor of the 19th century and the incandescent light bulb genius had no more than four months of formal school, yet he created and indelibly wrote his name on the sand of time for all to see; even generation yet unborn.

Mr. Henry Ford, the automobile guru and founder of Ford Motors, like his mentor, Edison had few months of formal education, yet made eternal impression on success and fame in the automobile industry. Many decades after Ford's death, till today Ford motor is still in the market and on the road! Henry Ford lives on.

Mr. Abraham Lincoln, the16th president of The United States, never had more than few months of formal education, yet accomplished so much: became American president, one of the most respected figures around the world. So many people still believe in his wisdom and intellect such that his quotes are still as relevant now as they were when first made decades ago- he lives on!

Mr. Walter Annenberg, the founder of Wal-Mart dropped out of Pennsylvania University after the death of his father to turn around his father's comatose business- and he did well. Today, Walter lives on, and two of his sons ranked the 9th richest billionaire in the world (2016).

We have dwell much in the past so it's time to be in the

present, and still prove the point with people of our time. In our present day we have Bill Gates, co-founder of Microsoft and the world richest billionaire with net-worth of $75 billion (2016), he is a Harvard University dropout.

Paul Allen, also co-founder of Microsoft and the 40th richest billionaire in the world (2016) with net-worth of $17.5 billion, he is a Washington State University dropout.

Mark Zuckerberg, the founder of the famous on-line social medium platform,Facebook.com and the 6th richest billionaire in the world (2016), worth $44.6 billion, is a Harvard University dropout.

Larry Ellison, the owner of Oracle and the 7th richest billionaire in the world, worth $43.6 billion (2016), is a University of Chicago dropout.

Sheldon Adelson, the 22nd world richest billionaire (2016), worth $25.2 billion is also City College of New York dropout.

Michael Dell, the owner of Dell Computers who was the 35th richest in the world (2016), worth $19.8 billion, is a University of Texas dropout.

Ray Kroc, founder of Macdonald eatery and pioneer of franchise business model, only had high-school diploma in salesmanship.

Tupac Amaro Shakur was a high-school drop-out, yet

he made enough money and fame, became first-rated rap song singer and writer, and died as the world best rapper at twenty eight.

The above listed dropout-turned billionaires are suprises and miracles to those who extol too much the ability of intelligence quotient test (intellectual ability) to predict the future success of people. They thought those who lack high intellectual ability (Those whose IQ test results or academic performance are low are doomed to failure)But the world billionaires have proven otherwise.

To be classified as "dropout" doesn't expressly say anything about the person's intellectual ability, though. It says the person didn't complete his/her school program, and so was not awarded certificate. It doesn't tell whether the person dropped because of lack of sponsorship, self-motivation, involvement in cultism, or just low academic intelligence. However, people insinuate dropouts dropped because of low academic performance. But this is not always the case.

But even if all dropouts have low IQ; some of them, especially the turn-billionaires have the most important and essential intelligence necessary to succeed outside the academia: emotional intelligence.

Intelligence is many; Gardner identified seven: linguistic, logical-mathematical, musical, spatial, body-kina esthetic, personal (i.e interpersonal and intrapersonal)

Contemporary psychologists proved other intelligence are crucial than IQ in determining what we become after school days.

Daniel Goleman, in his book *Emotional Intelligence* says "Academic intelligence has little to do with emotional life." He also posits that "At best IQ contributes about 20 percent to the factors that determine life success which leave 80 percent to other forces."

I am tempted to bring one more quotation as proof to the in-ability of IQ to predict the future success of people, Richard Branson, an astute entrepreneur, in his losing my Virginity, says "I once took an IQ test where the questions seemed absurd, I couldn't focus on any of the mathematical problems, and I think I scored about zero. I worry about all the people who have been classified as stupid by these kinds of IQ tests. Little do these people know that often these IQ tests have been dreamed up by academics who are absolutely useless at dealing with the practicalities of the outside world."

Evidently a whole range of emotional abilities: like being able to motivate oneself and others toward goal in the face of daunting challenges; resilience, delayed gratification, control of impulsive indulgence, empathy, keeping upbeat, and just thinking objectively and clearly are what we need for success in many fields and careers

The potentials of these more determining intelligences are down-played because they don't show up in IQ test, and as many psychologists admit; there are yet no standard means to measure emotional intelligence.

Those who do well and become successful in the world have what it takes to succeed in life after school: sound emotional intelligence; particularly an effective personal intelligence.

Personal intelligence which divides into interpersonal and intrapersonal are what make the difference in the future lives of people after school in wide spectrum of human endeavor, not certificates nor degrees. If a person has a disproportionately low academic intelligence but high and effective personal intelligence, nevertheless would do well, if not marvelously well in their field or business. Little wonder why dropouts suddenly surge into stardom and high social recognition if they utilize their strengths- personal intelligence. No woman asks for the certificate of her favorite hairstylist, nor make-up artist. No celebrant wants to know if his/her event planer has degree or certificate; what concerns him/her is "Make my ceremony the best within the much I can afford, and let attendees always remember this day for its fun and grand". No music or football fan ever asks to know if their best musician or player has certificate. I doubt if certificate would be of foremost importance in an audition into the film or movie industry as it is certainly the case in employment interview yet the film industry has brought so much to the table; both in cash and in social status of actor and actresses.

So many people who wouldn't have been known but for entertainment industry are millionaire celebrities –

thanks to the potentials of the other intelligences.

Almost all the success icons mentioned above are business people coordinating and harnessing the abilities of people to meet their goals and make profits. People who don't have interpersonal skills find it hard to survive in business environment; they don't know how to relate well with others, don't know how to motivate themselves and others toward goals; don't know how to even make short term sacrifice for long term benefit (Delayed gratification), don't know how to resolve conflicts among workers, or between them and others; would always have "Mine" mentality rather than "Our achievement" mentality; they would hold grudges and pride in high esteem over the business interest and survival. To summarize; they lack social skill. And unfortunately, business is a social activity.

A case in point is about a barber shop owner (A spinster) who allowed her barber (employee) to resign over the unruly behavior of her younger brother. This young brother apparently jobless was sent by her sister who owns the shop to meet the barber for the weekly rental charge. On reaching, he seated with customers to watch TV as customers waited for their turn. Another customer came but no vacant seat for him, so the customer reasoned that it will make sense if non-customer stand up for him so he could wait for his turn, and asked if everybody seated wanted to have haircut. The barber said all but the brother. With that the customer suggested the brother stand for him; he refused yet quarrel the customer to the point the customer was surprised at the brother's gut and unruly behavior, the customer asked who he was; not surprisingly he was the shop owner's brother. The customer left for lack of seat. The barber was angry at this brother for driving customer and asked him not to repeat this act. This infuriated the brother and he slapped the barber; asking "Who are you to talk to me like that." He probably thought, as a barber he is not qualified to correct him in his sister's shop.

The barber decided to resign but while he worked to complete the day's work, few hours later, the brother wanted to go, and he asked for the payment. The barber refused paying the young man and said "I won't pay you any money, go and call your sister." When the sister went the following day, she was unable to correct this arrogant act of her brother and settle them; she couldn't plead with the barber not to resign, rather she allowed the barber to resign.

But no barber would tolerate such, so she continued changing barbers intermittently till customers avoided the shop because of ineptitude at personal skills. If that brother were to manage a family business, he probably would literally stand on workers' head not minding who is hurt.

If the shop owner were to have an IQ rating above 100 she probably would do poorly in business irrespective of high academic intelligence.

Gardner crowns it all thus "Many people with IQ of 160 work (ed) for people with IQ of 100, if the former have poor interpersonal intelligence and the latter have a high one. And in the day to day world no intelligence is more important than interpersonal. If you don't have it you make poor choices about who to marry, what job to take and so on. We need to train our children in personal intelligence in school."

In all cases of success known to me, education is basic, not degrees. There are countless degree, and perhaps Ph.D. holders who are not successful at anything, and living from hand to month, so to speak! "Educated derelicts"

Education makes success easier to achieve, In our dictionary definition of education, we observed that it's a "process of teaching, training and development of skills". Though, the definition mentioned schools and colleges; it is because these are conventional institutions where teaching and training are done; which brings about improved skills, not because it is the only place we can be educated.

Education could also be gotten from any person or persons knowledgeable in what we need; whether in school or not- After all, Thomas Edison, after his three months formal schooling, his mother taught him the basics to master reading, writing and arithmetic. The boy, through passion for science, and self-development was able to read up many books and became one of the leading inventors the world has ever known.

The education needed for improving skills must not be certificated, but certificates and degrees are necessary for paid employment and political appointment.

The irrelevance of certificate(s) for success in business and personal life may be accountable for the success of school "drop-out".

The advantage of the drop-out over the illiterate is that drop-outs have acquired the basics Arithmetic, scientific and English knowledge needed to succeed in various fields, and as such can improve through self development and reading.

In contrast, the illiterate can't read about other people's work in their chosen field; neither can they read about other successful people's biographies which would have served as a model after which to follow. They also cannot put down their knowledge in an articulate and co-ordinate form to apply and build on, and above all, they wouldn't attend seminars, and may not value training.

With these obstacles to contend with, their road to success is more strenuous. However, this doesn't prevent them from success, if they have ambitious.

The main point of this chapter is to clear the misconception of many people, that for them to be successful, they must be a diploma, degree or Ph.D. holder. Rather, a basic education like SSCE or OND or their equivalent is all that's necessary. This misconception has deluded many to stock-pile degrees; thinking it will automatically make them rich or socially recognize, but most times are disappointed. This same belief makes some graduates waste five to ten years looking for job everywhere, instead of putting aside those piles of certificates, be creative and self-employed- they thought their success is in their certificates.

Success is not found in great universities and campuses, nor in the fame behind school names. Our present educational system had failed in creating success, and in particular wealth. All they produce is certificates of all types.

However, this should not be construed in any way as obliterating the importance of education in the search for success in whatever field; rather is to de-emphasize the focus on certificates.

Mr. Thomas Edison, Henry Ford, Walter Annenberg, Mark Zuckerberg, Michael Dell, and even Bill Gates of Microsoft all went to school, albeit, some, few months, others, few years of formal schooling: they did not complete, and so did not posses certificates —they were self-educators-they read loads of books, and practice what they learn.

Thomas Alva Edison himself made this statement as a testimony to his self-education: "my refuge was the Detroit Public Library. I started with the first book on the bottom shelf and went through the lot, one by one.

I didn't read a few books, I read the library". As he cast back his mind to 1862 when he was one of the earliest members of (this) public library, he recalled, he was given card number 33, and paid the substantial fee of two dollars ($2:00) for it as at then! Little wonder why he devoted a spacious room in his business empire to his personal library with over 10,000 books!

Former American president, Abraham Lincoln did similar thing about reading and self-education and development; Henry Ford too, and virtually all great men of history.

If anybody wants to be successful at any calling at all, he himself too must have basic education; be prepared to continually read, train and developed skills critical to success in his desired field.

So many people who claim to search for success never read through three to four books in their chosen field a year. Some have not read through any book since they left school, not to talk of attending a seminar.

How could such a person be successful? If you study the life of any successful person, you will attest that he/she is/was serious about attainment of goals. He gives his best to it, read loads of books, spend sleepless nights to learn the critical skills needed, and eventually master them.

Brain Sheer, author of *what rich people know and desperately want to keep secret* says "when it comes to success, the usual 8-9 hours is not enough", In related counsel, senior pastor of House of Dayspring

International Church, Pst. Sanjo Odunayo says "Successful people live their lives deliberately". I totally submit to their statements. If you must be successful, it must be by your choice and commitment.

For those who want to be successful in paid employment; they should cherish, and hold fast certificates of all sizes and colors, for in it, their appointments and promotions depend. Maybe, more important is the fame behind the institution which award the certificate –you know, your employer is more likely to rate a Harvard Certificate superior to any other certificates awarded by a Nigerian university- that is the belief.

Chapter Nine

CREATE A PLATFORM TO SHOW-CASE YOURSELF

Success is more about knowing and proving to people what you truly know: demonstrating to the world your ability. Whatever you know and keep secret; nobody else will know about, let alone appreciates and pay for it; the value of such knowledge is relevant to you alone, and so won't fetch you money-neither praise.

In the field of finance, there is a popular terminology known as "vehicle"- the tools used to make money. For the purpose of this chapter, I will call it "platform".

Platform is necessary to show-case your ability whether such platform is created for you, or you created it; what matters is "have a place to show-case your talent".

Talent is what gives us recognition as an individual. It helps to   show the abilities God had given to us, with which we can be of help and contribute to our world and be a blessing. Without talent, we are just like the next person. For us to get the best from it, we have to discover and hone it so that the full benefits are derived. It is true that everybody has talent; some are easily noticeable, such as talent for singing, dancing, artwork, and football playing; while some are subtle and need to be hunted for.

On the other hand, people-management skill, effective communication; conflict resolution and reconciliation, and ability to recognize subtle differences are difficult to recognize in people; sometimes, those who have them may not even recognize unless a proper evaluation is done.

This is where platforms to hone and show-case talent become indispensable.

Platform is where you discover your talent and make conscious effort to hone it to become better, through help of mentors, or others who are more experienced in the industry. They watch while you perform, and make objective comments and advice.

Because the mentors, panelists, or spectators may not know you personally, they could not give flattery praise or skewed judgment. Their constructive criticisms and well-meaning corrections can bring out the hitherto hidden better part of you!

As said earlier, platform could be created for you, or by yourself. Workshop and studio are platforms those in the "artwork or mechanics" can create for themselves.

There are different platforms for different talents. Ceremonies such as naming, birthday, or wedding are platforms for comedians; our streets are platform for up-coming pastors and evangelists; churches are platforms for pastors; football pitch is the platform for football players; night clubs, ceremonies, church choir, or studio are platforms for musicians. For craftsmen, their platform is their workshop. Online community members or forum, or user' group is a platform for writers and bloggers.

There are already some platforms created for those in the music, arts, and comedy industry by some socially responsible organizations and individuals. Platforms like *Project Fame*, hunting for musical talent, courtesy of MTN; *Dance with Peter Show*, for dancers, courtesy of GLO; *Land Mark Star Show*, courtesy of Land Mark Studio; *Stand up Nigeria*, comedy talent hunt, courtesy of Bunmi Davies; *Nnena Talent Hunt*, for children under the ages of 4 to 16 who can sing, play musical instrument, choreography, and acting, courtesy of Nnena and Friends of Wale Adenuga Production; *Most Talented Gospel Artist in Nigeria* (MTGAN);*Maltina Dance All Talent Show*, courtesy of NBL-Maltina; Nigerians Got Talent; Nigeria Idol ; Big Brother Naija; Voice of Nigeria from Airtel & Cocoa Cola etc.

The above mentioned platforms are the few, space can allow, however, it is up to you to know which will serve you better. I urge you research for more and choose anyone to bring your talent to stardom.

These are good platforms aspiring persons can take advantage of, and become who God had made them to be, and make a lot of money. Many talents have been honed in these platforms. Thanks to these organizers!

Stocks, mutual funds, annuities, and CDs are investors' vehicles (platform) for investing in the capital market.

Now, the big question is "what is your platform for honing and show-casing your skills?"

Until we come to terms with the reality of platform in success search, and make deliberate effort to create, or avail ourselves with the opportunities created by these platforms, we may still be some steps behind success.

Up-coming artist should avail themselves of these opportunities whenever they show up.

Chapter Ten

DELAYED GRATIFICATION

Delayed gratification is one essential attribute every genuine success seeker must develop and deploy deliberately to create success in whatever she/he does.

Many of us find it difficult to resist the temptation of early enjoyment. Many of us are immersed in the desire to quickly satisfy the seemingly pressing and urgent wants of today; we never know that if we don't learn to control the compelling urge of instant gratification of today's wants, more wants will certainly come up later, with little or no resources to satisfy them. It beats my imagination if people choose to eat-up their future today, and sooner than they could realize the future becomes the present, and with another problem; then they look for somebody to blame!

We are in generation when most of us still want to live like the prodigal son of the Bible who pressed for his inheritance, then return in short while after he lavished his share; seeking to be laborer in his father's house in order to have daily bread.

When some of us get money, the first thing we think is

"what will we buy", how do we spend this money so that people will know that we are this rich"- We want to keep up with the joneses: we want to show off. We want to prove to our neighbors how richer we are, but little did we know that our neighbors might even be richer but have chosen to delay gratification so when they begin the enjoyment, it will flow endlessly and effortlessly. Instant gratifiers don't know that the ability to take restraint in any activity when necessary even though, they are presently comfortable and impressed with their riches is a sign of maturity.

We only need to enter the credit department of any lending institution to appreciate how deep-rooted is the yarning for instant gratification, and the lending institutions are taking advantage of it.

The most worrisome thing is that most of these borrowings are to finance consumption, not investment.

Gone are the days when banks and other lending institutions strictly and meticulously scrutinize and appraise credit application for eligibility and risk factor associated with every credit applicant.

Also worrisome is the ease with which consumer loans are approved; you just need to be an employee of any recognized organization, and you can have it, anytime! I was very surprised when a brother who has barely served a year in an institution was given credit facility by a bank-when not yet vested (has not served a minimum of ten years), and I ask, should anything suddenly cut off his employment, from where will the bank recover its money.

In the past, credit applicants, especially civil servants must be vested before approval of any credit. The rationale being that a vested civil servant or company employee is entitle to pension benefit if the appointment is terminated, not sacked though, the bank can fall back on his pension benefits for the loan recovery.

I agree with Robert Kiyosaki, author of **Rich dad, poor dad** as he says that the financially savvy profits from the ignorance of the financially naive.

Lending institutions are actually profiting from the ignorance of these instant gratifiers; as they consolidate or continually role-over these debts all through the active working years of these borrowers.

However, credit or debt has its position in wealth building (leverage) I admit that for more than a year after building my house in Port Harcourt, I leveraged on debt to return back to my former financial status before the building; on fifty, fifty between financer and I. There is nothing bad in this case as it is termed investment debt; the profit pays for the loan, and even keeps left over for me. It is absurd and an abuse however, if used for consumption and ceremony (consumer debt instead of investment.)

Many cars and luxuries enjoyed by some civil, public

servant or company workers are cars or luxuries of the future; if not for loans, the owners could have only afford them in the future, but they pressed on for it now, and will sacrifice their future earning at the expense of future needs and investment opportunities.

I believe that if anyone must make and sustain money (wealth) he/she must have emotional intelligence in good dose, not physical strength.

Delayed gratification is necessary also in any other field, be it academia, music, entertainment, public speaking, craft or in the sporting industry. The celebrities in these industries have got their fair share of delayed gratification, be it in reading books, rigorous training and rehearsals: they have invested in themselves.

Chapter Eleven

OVERCOME PROCRASTINATION AND INDOLENCE

Procrastination and indolence are twin enemies of success. They are commonly found among failures: It demands no actions to procrastinate; only wishing and talking.

However, every successful person in whatever calling knows that he/she must convert his/her wishes into program for action; and only action produces positive result.

Procrastinators never get things done because they are always looking for an ideal time to act: the time when all conditions for success would be met; when they will do it once and get it right.

As you probably know, there is a level of happiness when you finish a task; also, with work, your health improves, otherwise your body atrophies, and the result is untimely death- This inactivity accounts for many retiree's death shortly after retirement from active service.

DANGERS OF PROCRASTINATION

1) **Inadequate use of Potentials and capabilities:** An average person is endowed with so much potential and capabilities that psychologists say many persons only utilize insignificant proportion of them. This belief or position of the psychologists is not mere assertion, it is real and proven in the lives of many great men/women, both of old and present generation: Thomas Edison, Albert Einstein, Timothy Barnerslee, Mary Slessor, Mother Theresa, Michael Faraday, Henry Ford, the Wright brothers, Jesus Christ, Aristotle, to mention but a few. These persons achieved enormous feat that confound most of us; make us doubt if they were mortal men with same blood and passion like ours. No doubt, they were; they lived on this earth, marry, bear children, had fears and hopes like every one of us. They achieved so much because they knew procrastination will always robe them of success, so decided to fight it squarely; never to allow it to dominate or rule over them. When you work on your goals continually, focusing on the desire to succeed and the benefit; pressing down on procrastination, the result is a better potential and capability. Achievements are attained only by making timely response to actions and plans that need to be done in the interest of the desired result, not in the interest of convenience, or feelings; there are times you don't feel like taking

an action for no apparent rational reasons, but you must if it is crucial to your success- It doesn't matter if the task is boring; if it needs to be done, then it must be done now, not later.

2) **Laziness and Indolence:** procrastination is the breeding ground for laziness and indolence; and as the Bible says in the book of the Proverbs: *"Yet a little sleep, a little slumber, a little folding of the hands to sleep: so shall thy poverty come as one that traveleth, and thy want as armed man"* Prov:10-11. With the comforting trick of procrastination, it is very easy to be caught in chains of postponement of task, then series of tasks, and then a project; all in the illusion of waiting for a more convenient or better time, culminating into lazy and indolent lifestyle. This is not good for success seeker. Successful people are always acting on things they need to, on timely manner; watching out for the next line of action, and so forth, until the desired result achieved.

3) **Reactive rather than Proactive Predisposition:** reaction is an action responding to an earlier effect or stimuli. To the procrastinator, the earlier effect is always a bad or unfriendly one, prompting immediate action to avert problems created by inaction. When a person reacts, in most cases, he or she cures rather than prevent problems or exploit

opportunities, and as you may know, it is the exploitation of opportunity that produces result, not curing problems; you can't afford to ignore all problems though, if it has appeared. On the other hand, pro-action is better; it serves to identify and utilize resources and opportunities by forestalling impediment on the way of desired result. Hear what Theron Q Dumont says in his *The Power of Concentration* on this subject "It is often the quickness of brain action that determines the result. One man thinks 'I will do it', but while he procrastinates the other goes ahead and does the work." With the life style of procrastinators, they are predisposed to lose of opportunities and reactive lifestyle. Procrastinators always live in the past, always trying to catch up with the past.

4) **Not Getting the Most from Information:** information too, is like money; it has time value, though instead of increasing with time, it reduces. This accounts for why some information needs rapid response to it; imagine the consequence of delayed action on security tip up, investment opportunity etc. Also picture a procrastinating author of ICT book or of other technology field spending, 12-18 months to publish a book. The value of the book at launching might have almost disappeared because of new technologies and inventions- It must have been obsolete because new

technologies, apps, gadgets etc must have been introduced, and as such has overtaken those in the book. Information Communication Technology (ICT) is one field that rapidly evolves within few months, even as few as six. So procrastinators would not get the most from information; they would delay action, and reduce the value of such information.

HOW TO OVERCOME PROCRASTINATION

The title of this chapter is "overcome procrastination and indolence". Urging you to overcome something without telling you 'how to' may not do you much good. That is why the "how to...." sub-title is necessary.

To overcome indolence, you already know "how to-just take action; and active person can't be lazy.

However, the big question will be how to overcome procrastination?

Here is the "how to"

1) **Don't wait for all resources** for a project to be complete before starting off. The wait for all resources to be complete before starting out on a project, in most cases, are the real cause of procrastination. Often times, the first step is all you need to overcome procrastination. Remember this popular adage *"a journey of 1000 km begins with a step"*

2) **Develop a positive mental Spirit:** You need positive mental spirit to overcome the sneaking inertia that culminates into real procrastination. It is true that the root-cause of some procrastination is the fear of poorly executing task. When you develop positive mental spirit, you always see more of your abilities than disabilities. To see more of ability than disability, actually creates and builds confidence in you, and overcome the fear of poorly executing the task. This has been discovered as the cure of some procrastination.

3) **Cultivate Decisiveness and Follow up with Action:** the Oxford Advanced Learner's Dictionary defines decisive as "able to decide something quickly and with confidence." When you cultivate decisiveness, you make quick, yet not shabby decision, and as such you trust your decision, and follow it up with action immediately. This quality mitigates procrastination.

4) **Make a Time Table:** make a time table of all critical activities in a project, and don't allow the scheduled time elapse without attempting it.

5) **Divide Activities:** divide every activity; especially the ones identified as subject of procrastination, into series of simple tasks to be

done one after the other. Dividing often procrastinated activity into series of simple tasks, make the activities simpler and more inviting to begin.

6) **Live Organized Life:** procrastination is part of everybody's life, but unorganized people procrastinates the most, and as a result achieve very little in life. If things are not organized; they are crammed, and collide with one another, which become a clog on activities, making the activities to be more boring and intimidating-ultimately ensuring procrastination.

7) **Create Sense of Urgency in your Activity:** The illusion that there is more time, or even better time tomorrow to do something is the main culprit in procrastination. If a person creates tight schedule and time frame for completion of any job, that sense of urgency will kick-start action, and procrastination would be overcome; most of the time, what we need is the first step, and before we know it, a whole lot of tasks have been accomplished. So don't give a single free time in scheduling your activities, if you want them done. Activity that has no dead line takes forever to get started, while the one that has 365 days deadline are mostly not started until 300 days are gone; at such time, the urgency is apparently visible and demanding that no one can do a nice job. Remember, deadline exists to

solve the problem of urgency. I think that is why Peter Ferdinand, Drucker said "work without deadline is work toyed with". It takes forever to start because of the illusion of enough time tomorrow. So when it comes scheduling your work or activity schedule like you don't have tomorrow to postpone to.

8) **Reward Yourself:** reward is a great motivator. Reward yourself regularly for starting and finishing an otherwise procrastinate work, and build your confidence that you can always get things done, and on time.

9) **Don't Postponed:** don't postpone any work that could be done today without additional cost implication, or short-changing of activities of higher priority.

10) **Kick-start your activity with the great motivators:** *fear* and *desire* are great motivators, depending on what circumstance you engage them e.g. the fear of embarrassment and disgrace from your creditor can motivate you to start action that will generate the needed money for the debt. On the other hand, the desire to own a car can motivate you to take action that will generate the needed cash, thereby overcome procrastination for you. So use any to overcome procrastination- base on your circumstance.

11)**Apply The FWF Principle:** FWF is acronym for "Feared work First". It says that you start your day's work with the tasks or work you fear most. If you list your day's activities as in your "to do" list, you find out that some tasks are more intimidating than the rest. Those intimidating activities are sure candidates for procrastination because you wouldn't want to stand the embarrassment from such complex work. When you apply the FWF principle, you start your work with the task you fear most. By always starting your work with the task you fear most, you soon become dexterous and comfortable with those tasks that were hitherto dreadful. I first came across this principle in Robert Allen's book, and I applied it on my most dreaded subject, mathematics. This made me know math than before, albeit elementary math. Later I deploy it to other areas. I urge you to try it – it works!

Chapter Twelve

HAVE POSITIVE PERSONALITY (CHARISMA)

"Even the most brilliant of persons needs to work with others to have his or her idea come to fruition. Long-lasting success can only be achieved by having rapport with those with whom you have a co-dependent relationship." – *Randy Gilbert*

Charisma is essential for success of any human endeavor because human beings are "social beings", and in particular, business as well as carrier is a social activity-It could not be done successfully in isolation! The truth about importance of pleasing personality could be confirmed if we notice that great and successful people usually have followers; some followers are sycophants though, genuine followership is voluntary response to pleasing and friendly attitude of yours by people around- the people whom your daily activities touch. Successful people know this basic truth about success, and deliberately create charming attitude daily through smile, respect for people –both young and old (because they know that respect is a reciprocal), self-control, love, truthfulness, and of course integrity.

They also know that they will eventually need the support and co-operation of people around them (rich or poor), educated or not; they don't look down on anybody. They know that a poor man with vision today may become rich tomorrow. They know that even in business, people do business with whom they like; they work for person whom they are comfortable with- those who will respect them for who they are, not braggarts. They know that their product or service might not be the best in town, but with love, people may endorse their product or service over their competitors' and that is a big plus for them.

They equally know and believe in the marketing truth: potential customers believe word (Testimonies of customers) customers than those of service providers who are apt to extol the quality of their product or service. They rather induce people to speak and advertise for them (good service provider) through making themselves genuinely acceptable to people through better service quality, and good public relation.

Good enough, if such person want to aspire to any political office, his or her odd for success at the poll is almost guaranteed! - He or she has unknowingly prepared for political career. Take a closer look at any successful person both local and international then the truth will be revealed.

Nelson Mandela, Fidel Castro, MahatmaGandhi, Mao, Benito Mussolini, Chief ObafemiAwolowo, Dr. NnamdiAzikiwe, Herbart Macaulay, Isaac AdakaBoro and Ken Sarowinwa are few examples of people with proven charisma.

JOHN S. MATTHEW

Chapter Thirteen

CHOICE OF MARRIAGE PARTNER AND FRIENDS

Choice is a critical thing in Lives of all beings and organizations. Correct choices are hallmark of the successful. They know that deciding to do a thing is impliedly deciding not to do another if mutually exclusive. Consequently, every of our today's reality is rooted in our yesterday's choices; it's unfortunate that we do not always have the fore-sight to aid our decisions; we only regret our wrong choices with painful hind-sight.

Successful people also know that the number of correct choices determine the height of their success, and so are careful, calculative, deliberate and selective in their choices –they analyze and weight the pros and cons of every choice – so to speak.

On the other hand, unsuccessful people seem to take no cognizance of the effect of their choices in life on their success-they don't just bother!

Little wonder why they marry and divorce several times, making children of different mothers, which in turn culminates into a major threat to their peace and longevity.

Every successful person is, or at least should be discerning enough to know that his/her choice of marriage is critical, and does have a lasting effect on his/her successsooner or later in life no matter the field. I must admit here that if not for the kind of wife I marry,my achievements wouldn't have in any way near what it is now; many a times she had to sacrifice her comfort and benefit for us to grow.Mrs. Chioma John issuch a blessing, and I'm ever grateful to God for her.

Instances and stories abound where wrong choice of marriage partner has led to untimely death of some prominent persons: Sampson of the Bible is a clear example.

Decision on marriage partner is one of typical decisions that many make in relatively few minutes of emotionally hijacked moment when their rational is constantly under pressure and obscurity from the emotional mind to make a long–term decision in a short time, and perhaps constrained environment–the result is long-lasting regret, and irreparable damage to their success.

Truly, a good marriage partner is instrumental to the success of spouse, no matter the field; hence the truth about the popular saying, "behind every successful man is a woman." A good spouse knows that he or she is complementary to the other, not competing; she also knows and agrees she is a 'help meet', not a trouble meet. Same is true of the man. It is equally true that some partners are 'trouble meet - pardon me for that personal adjective, you cannot find in your dictionary or thesaurus, anyway. If you are, or had lived with a nagging, cranky partner, you can easily understand my point; you will agree with me that often times, he or she would not allow you read or prepare for important task ahead which you should be pre-occupied with. Such unfriendly attitude will not allow you pray, attend to important meetings of your association or of worthy friends or not allow you budget your money, let alone to live within your budget, always making you to appear in one police station or the other; always making you to apologize to people for her misdeed- the list could be endless.

Anyone who has such partner cannot think straight and clearly; he cannot be productive at work; when economy is in down turn - and every economy does, he will be first in the list to sack or down size-out.

Even in his private enterprise he is likely to be synonymous with mediocre performance; mistakes, excuses, quarrels, delay in job delivery- the result is lose of customer, and consequently, inability to cover overheads and other business expenses.

It is difficult for any successful person to truly assert that he independently succeeded without the help of his partner; even your partner prayers and encouragement alone are big enough supports to get you through the dark moment of your career or pursuit.

Only your friends, of course, good ones, and family will stand by you in your "trying times", so you need to recognize this from the outset of your journey to success, and recognize their importance and contributions.

So if you are like me who have deliberately chosen a supportive spouse - glory to God! Cherish her always for she is indirectly contributing to your success.

Correct choice in marriage partner should be the first correct step of every-would–be successful person. If you are reading this book as a bachelor or spinster, and want to be successful in whatever career you may choose; be it pastoral, please, try as much as possible to be dispassionate while making this critical decision- don't let beauty be your guide; beauty will fade away with time. Don't let rich family background be your focus; riches do disappear. Don't allow parent pressure be your determinant factor- you will be the one to live with him/her throughout life, even when your parents might have all gone.

It is a pity that some poor choice makers marry out of pity, or as a reciprocal for gift given by the person wanting to be married. This is sign of weak emotional intelligence –don't let this happen to you. Make choice that you will always happy you did.

The same admonishment goes concerning choice of friends. I am sure you too have heard of the popular saying "show me your friend, and I will tell who you are".

Friends are like mirror in some ways; they show who we are, or at least how we intend to be. According to research conducted by Dr. David McClelland of Harvard University on 'the quality and characteristics of high achievers'. "Reference group": the people we always associate with, was found to be more important in determining people's success or failure than any other factor. 'Reference group,' in the above quotation is synonymous with 'Friends'. As a clue, you better be selective in the choice of friends you keep.

Know that in making friends we reserve the right to choose the one to keep and discard. I deliberately use that verb, "keep" to draw your attention to the fact that we can inadvertently make a wrong friend, but it is up to us, and for the interest of our career to choose which friend to keep; so we reserve the right to discard unworthy friends: the ones that have no vision, no goals, no worthy desires- the type always around to distract, or misdirect.

No one blames anybody for going in contact with an obscure, bad or nonentity acquaintance, but everybody blames the person who keeps bad company because it is his/her responsibility to keep and fire friends to be successful in career.

Once you have known a friend is not the right one for you, or the kind of person you want to become, then it is time to quit the relationship. If you remain in a relationship after being aware that the person is not right for you, then it is a sure sign of indecision, and indecision is the heritage of the unsuccessful.

STORY OF A WORTHY FRIEND

Let me quickly recognize some worthy friends as a testimony to the value of good choice of friends in success.

Sometime in the year 2005, I came in contact with a young, very energetic, discerning, perceptive but emerging businessman. Business brought us together, but little did I know that we undertake the same kind of business. The relationship began, and before long, I saw some nice qualities of a good business person in him, and decided to follow closely that I may learn from him, even though I was more elderly and educated. While the relationship continued, I wasn't getting any financial support; which made some friends advised that I quit the relationship saying "how can a man like that be your friend and doesn't help you financially", but I didn't mind, this was not weakness or indecision as many may misconstrue, but a strength and decisiveness; my target was not his money, but money-making skills and decisions.

I won't bore you with the details, but suffice is to say that he grew from level to level, and began to help me financially while at the same time rebuking me for some otherwise dangerous business decisions. He introduced and handed over to me some business contacts which as I write, are still viable contacts on my side. I was also striving to increase my customer base through prospecting for new, while maintaining old ones, and was growing until I got to the highest cash of my own. Meanwhile, I wanted to buy a car. When I told him about my desire for car, he yelled at me saying, "what do you need car for at your level, though, I bought my first car when I was 25, but you know that as at then I had finished building my my first personal apartment (3 bedroom flat) in Port Harcourt before I did that, do you want to be paying rent all through life? How much can you keep aside from the budget for the car that would be used to keep your business going". He rebuked, and I responded with my weak defense and tantrum. I left his house with anger, but his advice and warning haunted me till I changed my decision and bought a piece of land instead, which of course, was his advice.

Today, I too have finished building and living in my personal apartment-never to pay rent to anybody in my lifetime by the grace of God.

Needless to count, today at his 41 years, has raked much wealth in houses for rent, and for free to relatives, gorgeous cars grace his garage, active giver and benefactor to his church, and the executive director of his hotel, Raydes Hotels. At 41 and still growing, by the way, he is Mr. Macmillan Woha, aka:

Ogbakiri.

Mr. James Sakoroha, aka Father James is another worthy friend I came in contact with as a neighbor in Port Harcourt. An indigene of Bayelsa State, and a community health extension Officer. He came to pursue his degree in Physical and Health Education. Though, not as rich but an epitome of altruism – he actually carried me along.

When I discovered his qualities; and being convinced that I could emulate his good qualities that would help me in business, I made a commitment to be close to him, and I did! Even when a disagreement between us wanted to cut short our relationship; I didn't allow because I have seen qualities worthy of emulation in him: we maturely overcame, and moved on with the relationship.

When my business went under, and creditors were on my neck, he encouraged me to plead with them for time, and followed me to their houses; he was with me till the debts were paid.

His humility was away from the ordinary: he will proudly introduced himself at building site as a 'bricklayer' when soliciting for mason job, yet nobody suspected he was an undergraduate, earning monthly salary of seventy thousand naira (70,000) as at 2006, as an employee of The Ministry of Health.

At sites, he always insisted I serve him even when others would not want me to work with him because of my apparent lack of physical strength- they felt I was not strong enough to do manual labor, but I was.

His insistence on working with me at site made me stronger, and did provide for my daily bread in those hard times.

As I write, he has graduated, gone back to his state to totally immerse himself in the career of his choice (Health) as a deputy director in the Ministry of Health.

There are so many other worthy friends like Friday Okporo, Godwin Etuk, Onisogin Morris etc. there are also others I have discarded because they didn't fit into my vision. Have you done likewise?

These just concluded stories are testimonies that truly, good friends will make you, while bad ones will destroy. So be careful in the choice of friends you keep; they go a long way to determine who you eventually become!

Do you have the kind of friend that talks about and encourages reading, or the kind that encourages idleness, roaming the streets and partying or clubbing? Do you stick around friends that always seat by television to watch- the ones that the only clear and vivid narration they can give is about films they watched-Those who the only discipline and pain they can bear is to watch movies or soap opera, or the ones that never missed any live match on the screen? – beware!

I hereby challenge you to make deliberate attempt to evaluate your friends, and choose the ones to keep, and let the rest go. You should keep friends that have good moral up-bringing, good values system, good ambitions, good role models and mentors; the ones that talk about preferred future attainments and goals.

Do you believe that many are denied life-changing-opportunities because of the type of friends they keep?

To round up this topic, I bring to you words of my dear, senior pastor of House of Dayspring Church, Pastor Sanjo Odunayo; he says "successful people live their lives deliberately". Make your decision on the choice of friends deliberately.

SUCCESS IS NOT DISCREMINATORY OR PARTIAL

Why is it that many want success but only few attain that status as a "success"?

Could it be that success is discriminatory or partial, yielding itself to the beck and call of few persons alone, culminating to frustration and indigence of many? No. success is inanimate, lifeless, and insensitive, thus has no way to know whom to identify with, or favor.

Success has rules and principles to follow in order to achieve; that is why successful people, if they observe keenly the process of their success, see a pattern of orderliness of activity or activities that are critical to their success; they appreciate that they have done those critical activities or task well. With the awareness of doing those tasks well, they are sure that they could, or anybody else could repeat that success. This is the main reason success is taught and learned. Successful people all over the world are invited for speech, seminar, biography or autobiographies. Biographies of successful people are always sought after, so people who also want to be successful in their area could share in the secrete of, or the "how to story": success is clone-able.

Having established that success is clone-able, debunks any myth about partiality or discrimination of success. Success is like a track road that leads to water well; it could be straight and short, or long and windy; depending on your road and career. It is the person who has the discipline and resilience to pursue with commitment and purposefulness that gets it.

Studies have shown that successful people are disparate and heterogeneous in their skills, complexions, height, nationality, education, hobby, age, temperaments and passion; which made them chose, and succeeded in different field or career.

To further prove this, don't take this assertion for it. Check it out on books, biographies, or on Forbes magazine or site for yourself the world millionaires and billionaires in order to take your stand.

When I did my research on success, both on Forbes

and other success books, I discovered that Mr. Jeff Bezos, Founder of the most popular online book store: Amazon. Com worth $45.2 billion (2016)! From town called Little Havana, southern Florida.

Oprah Winfrey, Famous TV show hostess, born 1954 in Kosciusko Mississippi, worth $2.7 billion (2016)! What about Carlos Slim Helu, a Lebanese but Mexican descent who worth $ 73 billion as at when he displaced Bill Gates from his 13-year long occupancy of the world richest!

Yes! You heard me right; Bill Gates maintained this very exalted position of being the richest man in this wide planet for thirteen (13) consecutive years before his deposition, but now he is back as the richest man. This is no mean feat!

What about Mr. Warren Buffet, the oracle of Omaha and the founder and manager-investor who become the third richest man in the world worth $67.6 billion (2016).

Oh! Am very sorry for being carried away to the extent of mentioning only foreign and white people's success as if there were no successful black that has made it to the Forbes billionaires and millionaires mark, no. We also have billionaires and millionaires who have hit the Forbes magazine.

First, is the much revered, young, energetic Aliko Dangote of Kura town in Kano State, northern-western Nigeria; yes, he deserves to be listed first, after all he occupies the richest Black-man's position! Surely, this is no mean feat too. He worth $16.1 billion! What about his second: Mike Adenuga of Globacom that worth $4.7billion.

What about Bishop David Oyedepo of Living Faith Church World Wide. And now, the footballers: Mikel Obi, Odewingi, Kanu Nwankwo, Joseph Yobo etc.

Surely, some of the listed above have not been listed by Forbes as millionaires, or may not be listed; nevertheless, they have made success in their various endeavors to deserve mention.

I have restricted my list to these successful people because of space constraint, but suffice to give us the needed insight as to whether success is discriminatory or not.

In the above listed millionaires and billionaires, you see people of different races (White or Black), gender (male or female), age bracket, educational backgrounds, religious backgrounds and beliefs; divers up-bringing, and even different generations.

Note that Carlos Slim Helu was born 1943, now in his 70s (A Lebanese). While Aliko Dangote the grandson of Sanusi Dantata, was born in 1957 by Mohamed Dangote of town called Kura, in Kura Local Government Area in northern Nigeria, a Black, and a Muslim in his 50s.

What about Warren Buffet, the oracle of Omaha, and

CEO of BerkShire Harthaway. He is from Nebraska.

Surely, you must have heard of Ms Oprah Winfrey, an American Negro, in her early 60s.

Mr. Louis Odumegwu Ojukwu, was a successful importer of stock fish in and the richest man in Nigeria in his days; a Black and older generation.

Mr. Bill Gates co-founder of Microsoft, a year-two level drop-out of Harvard University. Richard Branson, the Virgin Air-billionaire also drop-out of school at the age of fifteen (15).

.

Mike Adenuga and Otedul, all Nigerian billionaires, of different ages and up-bringings. The list can go on and on, but it is okay.

If the above successful people were under a strict-same category for instance: all were White men, university graduates, or in their 60s or 40s; you probably could have excused yourself for not being equally fortunate to belong to that special class, but as you can see, they are disparate; ranging from graduates to university drop-outs, from Muslim to Christian to Jew, from married to singles, from Blacks to Whites, from Africans to Europeans to Americans, from software development to fund management, from manufacturing and industry to pastoring, and even to sporting; all walks of life.

However, there are few areas where successful people all over the world share common features and semblances; they are the "critical few". Have you heard of Pareto's 20/80 principle, yes, I guess.

They have these in common:

1) Vision: know what they want to accomplish in life
2) Perseverance or resilience: once they decide on an ambition, you better kill them with their ambition than kill their ambition (they remain resolute)
3) Keen perception: they see clearly into the future before the future becomes obvious for everybody to see
4) Industrious and good time managers: they recognize that no success can be achieved, or sustained with laziness and lousy management of time.
5) Passion: they don't make money their driving force for work; they know money will ultimately follow their passion.
6) Smart: good at mobilizing the needed resources to succeed.
7) Good marketing; they know good marketing is necessary to turn idea to cash.
8) Recognize God: they recognize God as their source of success..

Tell me what, if not for Keen perception, vision and resolution, would have made Bill Gates to drop-out of the much coveted business school of all time

(Harvard).

If not for vision, industry and smartness, what would have persuaded Walter Annenberg to drop-out of school on the death of his father when his late father's business was also dying at the time; why didn't he abdicate the management of his father's comatose business the way his siblings did, and maybe sell off the company to finish his education. He probably had seen what his siblings couldn't see. He also might have known that he has what it takes to turn around dying company like that, and he did!.

Okay, back home in Nigeria, why didn't Mr. Mohamed Aliko Dangote look for paid employment with his degree from University of Cairo, Egypt in those days when graduates in the country could literally be counted and virtually chose employment from their choicest Oil company or bank; vision, industry, and smartness.

In the early 80s when Bishop David Oyedepo started his million membership worldwide mega church. Why didn't he give up on the ministry when he was struggling to get off the ministry from ground; when he suffered aversion and rejection from people who would only follow when the church has got international recognition- vision, passion and recognition of God as his source.

These few listed people around the world have known and demonstrated that success in whatever field is not selective or discriminatory; just the discovery of principles, and commitment to remain resolute until it is achieved. It doesn't depend on the color of your skin, your age, your facial look, your nationality, degree, career or field; just know the essentials and live by them.

Successful people all over the world live by standard codes of conduct or tenets and value system. They are very discipline people, expert in managing their emotions. You too can make it to the-millionaire or success mark once you put these principles to test- it works!

JOHN S. MATTHEW

Chapter Fourteen

ARE YOU A STARTER OR FINISHER – BE BOTH

There are basically two sides to every coin; this is true and obvious to everybody.

This truth is evident in many things and activities of life: in business: profit or loss; in life: life or death; in competition: win or lose; and in many of our endeavors and aspirations: failure or success.

Every right thinking person would want profit from business venture, longevity from life, winning in contest, success in career, but sometimes the odd is unfortunately against our favor- we lose instead of winning, fail rather than succeed- it is pathetic!

In many of our endeavors; those that the outcome is largely dependent on us: business, education, relationship, project, career, you name them. Our results are determined by ability to keep the fire burning from start to finish- to keep the steam on till the last day.

TWO PSYCHOLOGISTS' CONTRIBUTION TO THIS CHAPTER

In many literary works as well as sourcing solution to man's enumerable problems, having a professional view is very important.

Thank God the survey conducted by two psychologists is readily cited in an article written by Dr. Heidi Grant Halvorsen on the internet **@https/hbr.org/2011/06/how-to-become-a-great-finisher** to provide us with the needed professional view.

Dr. Heidi Grant Halvorsen, in her article on "how to become a great finisher", identifies "staying motivated" from the start till the finish of project as critical to the completion of any project. She quoted how research conducted by two psychologists, Minjung Koo and Ayelet Fishbach helps to reveal why sustaining motivation is difficult, but however, suggested method of curbing this difficulty.

She said the psychologists found that the direction of thought affects motivation to finish. They identified two directions of thought which they termed: the "to – date thinking", and the "to-go thinking". They posit that if a person undertaking a project focuses on the progress made till date-the to-date thinking, the person would have complacency resulting from premature sense of achievement. In contrast, if another focuses on how far to go- the "to go thinking"; this thinking points to the gap between the goal's achievement and the present position and stimulates action necessary for completion.

She substantiated this position with studies conducted by these psychologists on college students studying during exam saying that the students were very motivated to their preparation when informed that they have 52% to cover their scheme of study' than when told they have achieved 48% completion of their scheme. They concluded by saying that the to-date thinking tries to create sense of "balance" in achievement by turning to other goals without completing any: a little of this here, a little of that there; which is the main weakness against accomplishment (and this they described as "classic good starter", not finisher).

"I'm not excusing myself but if I could have seen the shore I might have made it". This was a statement of regret by Florence Chadwick when she realized that she could have been on the California shore in few minutes which was less than half a mile, had she continued with her swim.

Florence Chadwick in the morning hours of July 1952 was determined to be the first woman to swim across the Catalina River (about 21 miles apart). Armed with enthusiasm and strong–will, she dived into the water and headed for the shore of California. Her mother together with her coach in a boat as she went side by side with them cheering her up, but the fog wouldn't let her see how close she was to the California shore- her target.

After much progress, but yet to finish, she demanded to be taken off the water, and was taken off. Shortly afterwards she discovered she was very close to the shore-hence the above statement.

Her statement indicates that if she was able to see the end (the to-go thinking) (4% to finish: less than a mile to go, of 21 miles) she would have been motivated to finish. With this story, I also endorse the validity of the to-go thinking to be a finisher.

So to succeed at any endeavor, in as much as it is good to have a high spirit when starting out, it is equally good to forge ahead to defeat any temptation compelling or harassing us to give in on our goal. Certainly we would meet challenges on our way, but we should be wise and strong enough to endeavor to complete our project because in completion lies winning and success.

It is clear from all indications that we have better "starters" than "finishers", yet we need both to succeed at any life endeavor.

You wouldn't be wrong if you blame the large number of abandoned projects, mediocre performance, failures in business and in life on the lopsided and disproportionate disparity of "starters" to "finishers".

Starters are known for lush ideas, sheer optimisms, quick to begin, hasty judgment, enthusiasm and of course, quick to abandon the novelty project and jump over to a seemingly fresher and better scheme.

On the other hand, finishers thrive in details and diligence; concern about the end product or completion, save the credit of the task to successful completion; they want to see their effort or contribution yield the desired result, know and believe that no matter how good the beginning of a project, if it is not completed, then it is a failure.

One major problem with starters is their inability to anticipate and perceive the future. When they conceive an idea or embark on a project, often are novelty, they usually are enthusiastic and probably overzealous and consumed with the quick take off and the positive outcome that they undermine the importance of thinking through the future in which the project or plan will be executed.

Thinking through the future of any project is critical to the success of any project, because it is in the future the activities or plans would be executed, and one thing they didn't know, or they know but ignore, is that nobody has crystal ball through which to clearly and rightfully see the future; they must try to think through and anticipate- the future must, at least be slightly different from today; their sheer optimism can't help failure.

Optimism, psychologists would argue that it is an energizer to human beings, enabling us to embark on our activities- granted. But sheer optimism does not, and cannot replace careful and critical analysis of facts and details of project, career. And inability to deal with details is what stalls many projects.

It doesn't matter how boring or detestable is detail to anybody, if it is critical, as it is always in many endeavors, the person must deal with it if he or she really wants to finish, and you can't succeed at anything unless you finish.

What many starters fail to recognize is that project, career or any worthy pursuit comprises many activities, and these are various levels of complexities and skills requirement, hidden in those complexities are challenges of various degrees and natures that must be surmounted to continue, and to win.

If they are not able to surmount the challenges, they stall, become frustrated and consequently abandon the project.

Since challenges are part of life, challenges are to be expected and prepared for in advance; when it eventually surface, then of course it is time to face it with appropriate skill required to deal with.

When faced with challenges requiring higher skill and ability than you have, as it sometimes would because no one has all it takes to deal with all challenges, the only wise thing to do is to ask for the service of the one who knows; let him clear the challenge, then you can take over afterwards.

Success in many human activities is largely a team work. (it will be to glory of all who contributed (typist, publisher, authors whose works are cited, and of course, the author's) if this book sell. Therefore it is foolish for anyone to deny himself the help of others, just because he wants to arrogate to himself all glory of the success. Such would be an indescribable greed, and a classic case of "one being the architect of one's failure".

Recall the story of R.U Darby and his uncle on the chapter "Can You Identify Success, Even Though Far Off?"

As the story goes:…when the vein of gold disappeared with their hope, instead of to sought after the service of the person who knows (fault line engineer, in this case) to surmount the challenge, they sold the machinery to a junkman who probably, out of wisdom or intuition, sought after the service of fault engineer, and finally discoverer gold (success) Darby's uncle failure, however, may neither be-attributed to foolishness nor greed, but certainly to ignorance and frustration.

JOHN S. MATTHEW

Chapter Fifteen

AVOID SHORT CUT

I know, to many of us it is very difficult to heed this advice, especially when things are seemingly tough and unresponsive. Short cut, aka cutting corners is very appealing to us in this generation of instant gratification, and instant results: time is of essence to us all; and everybody seems running out of time and patience.

People no longer want to pay the price for the success they desire; they want to get good grade at school, but can't put in quality time to study; they want to be rich, but can't resist buying "articles of wealthy appearances" (the show off mentality); wanted to be famous but can't put in the years and effort the famous person has put-so the smarter ones prey on them: they are swindle with every fast solution, and "get rich quick" scheme.

Genuine and lasting success in any field is an indication that the person has paid the price.Study the biography of any successful person in history: Henry Ford, Thomas Edison, Albert Einstein, Jeff Bezos, Bill Gates, the Wright Brothers, Lary Page, Sergey Brin, Nelson

Mandela, Mahatma Gandhi, Dangote, Bishop Oyedikpo, David Ibeyemeiye, Mike Adenuga, Oprah Winfrey you will agree with me they have all paid their prices. They were not born famous, most of them started from a humble beginning –putting in longer hours than resting-pressing on to their desired goals.

Hear from the richest black himself (Mr. Aliko Dangote). "I built a conglomerate and emerged the richest blackman in the world in 2008, but it didn't happen overnight. It took me thirty years to get to where I am today. Youths of today aspire to be like me, but they want to achieve it over-night. It is not going to work. To build a successful business, you must start small and dream big, in the journey of entrepreneurship, tenacity of purpose is supreme".

True, short cut is irresistibly appealing especially now that time seems our scarcest resource. However, I doubt if it will please anybody, after hurriedly bypassed steps to arrive at a destination or goal early but only to be forced or even compelled to go back to those steps because they are too critical to success as to allow short cut that could nullify any purported success- double work! People are demoted, certificates withdrawn, admission cancelled, work contract revoked if found afterwards that credentials or other documents are falsified or fraudulently obtained- it is a shameful experience, and I don't think you will like such experience, avoid short cut!.

When tempted to take short cut think of the dangers below: THE DANGERS OF SHORT CUT. Those who give in to the alluring temptation of short cut have to deal with the following problems:

1) **Undermine their value and Integrity:** values and integrity are moral guides to conscientious actions of men. When people don't have any values or integrity to direct their free-will, soon drift to permissive life, and that can be dangerous to themselves and others in general. Values like hard work, honesty, orderliness, respect for human life and elders; also integrity of your family name, community name, club name or association should not be down- played or undermined even in our quest for success in life.

No genuine happiness or sense of accomplishment could result from ill-gotten wealth. No matter how stupendous, it can't tame the continual reminder of guilt for killing or robbing a person in order to take over his/her wealth.

What about the beautiful girl who trades her body for high marks in examination rather than discipline herself to learn and pass examination.
If she passed and graduated with upper division, will she be bold and proud with such success wherever she goes? Probably not; can she defend her certificate when employed? May be not; can she be happy about her inability to defend it? Certainly not. Then what is the value

of an achievement if it doesn't give joy. Isn't the joy of winning legitimately, and the self-assertive statement "I did it, "is what make objective worth pursuing in the first place?

Some pastor in quest for large congregation and fame, and fat offering seed stops at nothing to seek power from diabolic means (short cut), yet courageous enough to claim they are healing and performing miracles in God's name – instead of spending quality time with God, seeking his presence, favor, and learning how to hear Him.

Let me say here that those who undermine their values have to deal with their guilt throughout their lives.

Many people in the circular world are deluded to believe the popular saying "The end justifies the means" I hope you are not part of that park. The end does not justify any means. Does successfully swindling a man (end) justify the act of swindling him? The Holy Bible has expressly stated: "Be not be deceived; God is not mocked: for whatsoever a man soweth, that shall he also reap". Gal 6:7.

2) **You miss the knowledge and experience:** Every worth-while achievement comes with knowledge and experience. Their knowledge and experience are by products of the means of achievement. If anybody follows short cut to

achievement, he definitely miss out on the knowledge and experience the other person who didn't take short cut has.

For instance, the graduate who paid somebody else to write his project does not have the knowledge and experience of project writing even though may have his certificate. He should be ashamed and feel empty if a younger brother or sister, believing (s)he is a graduate and has written project approaches him/her for guidance on project writing- think about it for a moment. Also, what will a person with ill- gotten wealth offer on mentorship, can he really mentor himself?

3) **In case it back fire.** Avoid short cuts, in case it back tire. And it does, often than not. Often time we feel smarter and wiser than the other person or system, and would want to beat the system simply because we were lucky or some other person was the other day. Little did we know that while every day has 24 hours, no two days are absolutely the same; hence the uncertainty of tomorrow: the luck that was available the previous day might had gone today.

Picture a real life situation in which an importer, instead of going through the normal payment and clearing process at the wharf, decided to short-cut his goods through the assistance of a dishonest custom officer to get the goods into the country through back door. After plans between them have been perfected, only for the custom officer whom he planned with to be sent on compulsory and urgent assignment by his boss!- deal back fires, so the goods impounded and the importer jailed. Remember the song of the iconic late reggae star, Peter Tosh: "You fool the people some time, but you can't fool all the people all the time---".

Think of another scenario where you got to an ATM (Automated teller machine) line for quick cash withdrawal but to your greatest detest and impatience, the queue was fairly long, and you decided to beat the queue by a ploy that didn't work. After much persistence on making it to the front to no avail; you had no option than to go back to the queue and take your supposed position, but this time with another catch which you inadvertently created by first wasting time at the front, trying to maneuver your way: many people have joined the queue continuing from your supposed (original) position and they didn't let you in on your otherwise original position. You were left with yet another ugly choice to go behind the last person on the queue. To add insult to injury; money got finished before your turn!-bad lesson and regret. So you see, avoid short-cut because it sometimes backfire.

4) **Jail term or Untimely Death:** In many societies, short cuts are mostly classified as illegal dealings, and illegalities are fast-lane drive to jail and untimely death. You would agree with me that many inmates are convicted on illegality count charge–obtaining something by false pretence, misrepresentation and the likes. These are speed-lane to jail. Many die in prison, or released after serving their terms to see the reality that their mates outside prison gate have got better achievements than they. Please, for the sake of your life, your success, your value, and the sake of your family name, avoid short cut.

Chapter Sixteen

TAKE ACTION

Congratulations! You have come a long way with me on this all important journey of life; searching through pages of this book for the principle of success.

I will say that success in whatever field has two basic segments: the knowledge acquisition, and the action taking segment; both are equally important. If you had painstakingly read through all pages of this book, and maybe other books on this subject, thank you. But you still need to do the last, single thing: take action. Action alone brings positive results, rewards, proofs that you indeed know what you claim to have learnt.

Many success and wealth books I have read, concluded by clearly asserting that irrespective of how many times you read through the pages books, without taking action concerning the things you have learnt, you can't succeed. This is very true, and may be is apt for me to even state more strongly that no success book is worth its claim of credit without a chapter calling for 'Action'- compelling readers to practice what they have learnt.

Hence the Holy Bible says: "Be not the hearer alone,

but the doer...." James 1:22. Consider another quote from Zen Saying "To know and not to do is not yet to know." Consider this also: knowledge is of no benefits to the owner, except that which he benefits from its use.

The Benefits of Action

Taking actions; especially positive actions, have profound benefits on life, and success in particular.

Through action to ascertain your capability in certain areas, you become sure by proving out yourself.

Sometimes it could be very unbelievable that we fail in little thing that we often take for granted and concluded we could do very well, but to our greatest surprise, we founder.

My brother, a graduate of marketing, and holder of diploma in computer from Admas Computers was surprised and embarrassed at his inability to connect desk top pc system (monitor, processor, and keyboard) to the electric power socket to power the system. Not being able to connect the individual component of the system together, he stalled and wasted his time trying to do what he has not previously done but have only read about. Since he couldn't connect the system, he was unable to proceed to the next phase of the interview: typing and saving document which he definitely knows well through practice (Action). This ugly scenario was a real life situation in which my brother found himself at a recruitment interview conducted by the Rivers State

Primary Health Management Board. He was to connect, type. and save documents, but he failed. Even I myself used to find it challenging to use computer at the cyber café, because of different browser setting and other related differences from laptop, which I regularly brows and do other things. This inability had embarrassed me several times till when I decided to take action to master using the cyber cafe, in case of any eventuality. Since that decision I repeatedly go to the cafe even when I have data on my modern to use at home, and now I am better and more comfortable at it. Action has paid off!

However, to another man from my community who also attended same interview, got it right because he owned a business center, and as owner of business center he must have at several times connected and reconnected pc, and also had type and saved document often in his business center. This was a big advantage "action" gave this man over my brother.

With this singular advantage, the young man passed the interview and got the job. As I write, he works with the Rivers State Primary Health Management Board; that is how powerful knowledge combined with action can be!

No action, no real experience. Real experience: the one that can transform; comes only from taking action (by doing). Those who have tried their hands on many things have got a lot of experiences – both good and bad, and all experiences are valuable for success.

No action, no positive result. Action begets result, that is why many things or courses we learn have the practical side, and without the practical you won't qualify or graduate. For instance, every medical doctor has done mandatory internship before being certified as medical doctor.

The same is true of lawyers, they must pass a mandatory one year of law school before called to bar. Only when a lawyer is called to bar is he qualified to defend a client in court.

Also, you can't be a lab scientist without having done enough practical. This is true of almost every area where success or excellence is needed. You can't be a pilot by only reading books; it doesn't matter how brilliant you are, you need the practical to fly safely. This example could go on and on, but suffice is to say that you can't excel in anything by merely reading books or taking instructions without putting into practice what you have learnt or have been taught – no positive result, and no success.

Many have read enough books, attended many seminars, listened to loads of tapes and instructions, but no result to show for it because they don't complement what they read or listened to, with action – it is time to swing into action, for good.

BIBLIOGRAPHY

1. Lahaye, Tim. *Why You Act the Way You Do.*Benin City: Nig. Joint Hiers Pub, 2002

2. Allen. Robert. *Multiple Streams of Income.* New York: John Wiley and Sons Inc. 2000

3. Fayemiwo, AdemolaMoshood, and Neal Margie Marie. *Aliko Mohammed Dangote: The Biography of the Richest Black Person in the World.* Houston: Texas. Strategic Book Publishing and Right Co. 2013

4. Hill Napoleon: Revised and expanded by Pell Arthur R. Dr. *Think and Grow Rich.* London: Vermilion, 2004

5. Allen, Robert. *Creating Wealth.* New York: Simon and Schuster. 1983

6. Tracy, Brian. *Goals!* Benin City Nig: Joint Heir Pub. 2003

7. Drucker, Peter F. *Managing for Result.*New Jersey: Montclair. 1964

8. Carson, Ben. Dr. *Take the Risk.* n.p Zondervan, 2008

9. *World Greatest Biographies.* USA: Reader's Digest Association, Inc. 2001

10. Sher, Brian. *What the Rich People Know and Desperately Want to Keep Secret.* Benin City: Nig. Self-Improvement Publishing. 2000

11. Newman, *Bill. The Road to Success.* Benin City: Nig. Marvelous Christian Pub. 1995

12. Goleman, Daniel. *Emotional Intelligence: Why it Can Matter More Than IQ.* New York: Bantam Books. 1995

13. Grant, Heidi, HalvorsenDr.*How to Become aGreat Finisher.* https/hbr.org/2011/06/how to become a great finisher.

14. Kiyosaki, Robert.

15. Barker A. Joel. *Paradigms:* The Business of Discovering the Future. New York: Harper Collins Publisher Inc.1993

16. Dumont Q Theron. *The Power of Concentration:* The Master Key to Achieve Anything in Life Faster and Easier: Benin City. Kingdom Life Publication. 2005.

17. Branson,Richard.*Losing my Virginity:* New York. Three Rivers Press. 1998.

ABOUT THE AUTHOR

Mr. John Samuel Matthew (Enumakinye) is a writer. He presents seminars on success and financial freedom. He owns the blog: enumaking.blogspot.com.ng.